JUST ~ IN ~ TIME

A Global Status Report

Chris Voss & David Clutterbuck

YLDS

IFS Publications, UK
Springer-Verlag
Berlin · Heidelberg · New York · Tokyo
1989

British Library Cataloguing in Publication Data

Voss, Christopher, *1942-*
    Just-in-Time: a global status report.
    1. Manufacturing industries. Management. Techniques: Just-in-Time
    I. Title   II. Clutterbuck, David, *1947-*
    658.5

ISBN 1-85423-038-7   IFS Publications
ISBN 3-540-51011-7   Springer-Verlag Berlin Heidelberg New York Tokyo
ISBN 0-387-51011-7   Springer-Verlag New York Heidelberg Berlin Tokyo

© **1989 IFS Ltd,** 35-39 High Street, Kempston, Bedford MK42 7BT, UK
and **Springer-Verlag** Berlin Heidelberg New York Tokyo

Phototypeset by GCS, Leighton Buzzard
Printed and bound by Short Run Press Ltd, Exeter

Contents

Preface

This book has been written for executives, from *all* functions, in manufacturing companies, who are concerned with how they can improve their companies' overall performance. An increasing number of companies have begun to adopt and implement a new set of manufacturing practices. These practices, known as Just-in-time management (JIT), were originally developed in Japan and have now spread throughout the world. Despite fear that the Japanese methods were embedded in their culture, Western companies have now learnt how to adapt these to their local environment and to implement them successfully. This book has been written with a number of objectives in mind:

- To bring together the experience of companies, world wide, who have successfully adopted JIT. The book starts with Japan, with Toyota who developed JIT, as well as looking at Japanese companies in diverse industry sectors. JIT has now been implemented world wide and the book looks at the implementation experience of companies in the US, UK and Europe.

- To show, through the use of diverse case examples, how senior managers have led JIT implementation and how JIT has resulted in major improvement in business performance.
- To show how JIT can be applied in a wide range of industries. JIT started in the automation industry, but it has now been applied in industrial sectors as diverse as aluminium and musical instruments.
- To identify the major implementation problems that have been encountered and to provide guidelines to help managers to start successfully and to lead a JIT programme.
- To identify the many myths and misunderstandings associated with JIT.

We hope that this book will do the above and more, and will lead to substantial improvement of business performance by manufacturing companies in the West.

Chris Voss
David Clutterbuck

1. JIT: a revolution in customer care and manufacturing cost reduction

Manufacturing and, increasingly, service companies determined to prosper in the 1990s must make radical improvements in productivity and flexibility. Just-in-time (JIT) is an approach that is enabling many companies, large and small, around the globe to do just that. In this introductory chapter, we explore what JIT is, why it is so important, and what prevents more companies making use of it.

1 JIT: a revolution in customer care and manufacturing cost reduction

The new competition

The competitive battles of the 1990s will be fought not only on cost and quality, but with an added dimension, that of speed and responsiveness. Joe Blackburn of Vanderbilt University, a leading US manufacturing expert, argues that time is displacing cost as the critical dimension of competition in manufacturing. This new area is becoming known as 'time-based competition'.

Over the last 20 years, Japanese corporations, originally led by Toyota, have developed new forms of manufacturing with the capability of responding rapidly at low cost and high quality. This is generally known in the West as 'Just-in-time manufacturing'. The Japanese had the vision to see a new form of competition emerging out of these new approaches. Initially in Japan, and now globally, the Japanese have been fighting on the time-based competition battleground. This book is designed to help senior management understand the nature of these new approaches and to show how they might be implemented. George Stalk, of Boston Consulting Group, who has studied this area in depth, argues that companies which are competing effectively on time-based competition are:

- Growing much faster and more profitably than their competitors.
- Becoming closer and more essential to their customers.
- Taking leadership positions in their industries.

There have been many attempts to explain why so many Japanese manufacturers achieve superior performance in terms of cost, delivery times and product quality. For a long time they tended to focus on aspects of Japanese social and working culture, on low rates of pay (which in fact, is very far from the case) or on the degree of automation. Attention then focused on specific techniques, such as quality circles, which were adopted in many cases in a piecemeal manner, and hence frequently failed. For all of these reasons, Western companies were able comfortably to ignore the lessons that were being painstakingly learned in Japan. Comfortable ignorance is no longer tenable, for a number of reasons:

- It is now clear that the success of Japanese manufacturing companies is due in large part not to individual, specific techniques or cultural factors, but to a philosophy of manufacturing that demands and embraces a wide range of techniques. Some of these techniques are well known and used in the West; others are not. Collectively, they have come to be called *Just-in-time* (JIT).
- The size of the productivity gap is still immense. Fig. 1.1 shows recent productivity levels in various countries.
- Competitive pressures on manufacturing industries of all kinds require constant and radical cost *reductions*. Some multinational

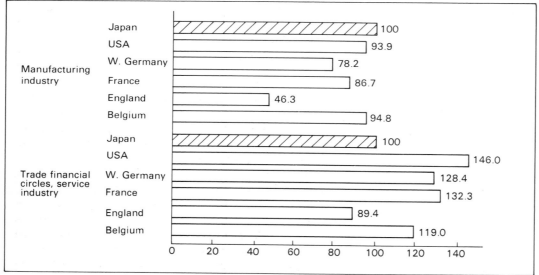

Manufacturing industry	Japan		100
	USA		93.9
	W. Germany		78.2
	France		86.7
	England		46.3
	Belgium		94.8
Trade financial circles, service industry	Japan		100
	USA		146.0
	W. Germany		128.4
	France		132.3
	England		89.4
	Belgium		119.0

Fig. 1.1 International comparison of labour productivity

manufacturers are now specifying expected levels of annual cost reduction to component vendors, typically of 1½% or more a year. Traditional methods of cost reduction cannot deliver.

● With the increasing movement away from competition based on price alone, to competition based on a broad set of factors such as quality and 'time-based competition', customers are increasingly demanding:

- ● Shorter, more reliable delivery lead times.
- ● Shorter design to delivery on new products.
- ● Increased product quality and reliability.
- ● Responsiveness on a wide range of dimensions.
- ● Ability to deliver high variety at short notice.

This has major implications for market share both locally and globally. The Japanese are delivering this in the marketplace. Figures research by John Parnaby of Lucas plc illustrate some of these performance measures in the electro-mechanical components industry (see Table 1.1). To compete in global markets, Western companies must match this performance.

Table 1.1 Performance measures in the electro-mechanical industry (Source: J. Parnaby, "A systems engineering approach to fundamental change in manufacturing." 9th annual IE Managers Seminar Manual, © Institute of Industrial Engineers)

Performance indicator	Japan	Western
Sales per employee per annum	$150k	$85k
Sock turnover ratio	15	5
Radio indirect : direct labour	1:2	3:2
Lead times (development and manufacture	50%	100%

● Product life is decreasing. In the early 1970s, a technically advanced product in, say, consumer electronics, would last 15 years, with gradual adaptation. Now product life may be as short as 15 months (see Fig. 1.2). In some cases, the product development cycle is longer than the product lifetime. This basic trend of reduction in product cycle affects or will affect virtually all manufactured goods. Traditional manufacturing approaches, with their long lead times to implement change, cannot cope. For example, many European car firms introduce a substantial model change once every 5–10 years. Some Japanese firms, such as Honda, have model lives as short as 3 years.

● Companies are finding it increasingly difficult to implement strategies because of the inertia within their organisations. One source of inertia is the inherent inflexibility of a typical manufacturing system. Once installed, a manufacturing plant is often treated as immutable, not to be changed substantially during its economic life. The opposite approach is illustrated by the example of a US factory which had embraced JIT. This factory treated machines 'as if they were on wheels'. If new strategies, products or changes in mix arose, the layouts and machines were moved rapidly to enable strategic changes and improvements to be implemented effectively.

JIT represents the antidote to many of these problems. It is not, of course, a cure-all, but it does permit companies to make continuous and significant improvements in all these areas, and in particular, in:

● Work in progress (WIP).
● Increased flexibility.

*Fig. 1.2 Product life cycles during the 1970s and 1980s (Source: H. Yamashina, "JIT in Japan: what can we learn from their experience." **Proc. 2nd Int. Conf. Just in Time Manufacturing**, IFS Conferences, 1987)*

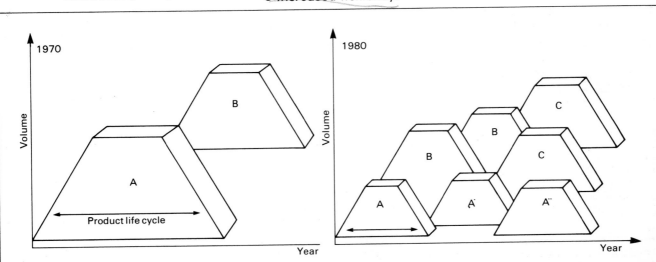

- Raw materials/parts reduction.
- Increased quality.
- Increased productivity.
- Reduced space requirements.
- Lower overheads.

These improvements are achievable in the West as well as Japan.

The scale of improvements companies can achieve is illustrated by these results from major manufacturing companies:

- Inventory reduction

Such results are not exceptional. Manufacturing companies in a wide spectrum of industries – from heavy to food processing – have achieved significant improvements in competitive position as a result of investment in JIT.

What is JIT?

Fuller descriptions of JIT are given at a later point in the book, but a useful working definition is given below.

The concept

JIT may be viewed as a production methodology which aims to improve overall productivity through the elimination of waste and which leads to improved quality. In the manufacturing/assembly process, JIT provides for the cost-effective production and delivery of only the necessary quality parts, in the right quantity, at the right time and place, while using a minimum of facilities, equipment, materials and human resources. JIT is dependent on the balance between the stability of the users' scheduled requirements and the suppliers' manufacturing flexibility. It is accomplished through the application of specific techniques which require total employee involvement and teamwork.

The elements of JIT

The fundamental aim of JIT is to ensure that production is as close as possible to a continuous process from receipt of raw materials/ components through to shipment of finished goods. Some of the elements of this system are as follows:

- *Flow/layout*. The physical layout of the production facilities is arranged so that the process flow is as streamlined as possible; i.e. for each component, the proportion of value-added time is maximised, the proportions of queueing and non-value-added time are minimised. The flow is analysed in these terms and the layout configured accordingly, resulting in the reduction and/or elimination of stores and conveyors; U-shaped or parallel lines may be applicable.

- *Smoothed line build rate*. This should be consistent with the process flow, i.e. as smooth as possible. JIT systems often try to smooth the build rate over a monthly cycle.
- *Mixed modelling*. A JIT objective is to match the production rate to order demand as closely as possible. One method of doing this is to increase the flexibility of production lines to allow the concurrent assembly of different models on the same line.
- *Set-up time reduction*. The object of reducing set-up times is to enable batch sizes to be reduced. Some companies aim to achieve a batch size of one.
- *Work in progress (WIP) reduction*. In JIT, WIP reduction is used to highlight production problems previously shielded by high inventory levels; these have to be resolved without delay in order to maintain production.
- *Kanban*. Kanban is a pull system of managing material movement, which comprises a mechanism which triggers the movement of material from one operation through to the next.
- *Quality*. The achievement of high quality levels is a prerequisite of successful JIT. Commonly used quality programmes in support of JIT include zero defects, statistical process control and work team quality control.
- *Product simplification*. This can be achieved by two measures, the rationalisation of the product range and the simplification of the method of manufacture by, for example, using fewer and common parts.
- *Standardised containers*. The use of small standardised containers to transport components.
- *Preventive maintenance*. Effective JIT requires the removal of causes of uncertainty and waste. A major cause of uncertainty is breakdowns; JIT programmes are normally supported by preventive maintenance.
- *Flexible workforce*. In order to support the objective of matching the production rate as closely as possible to order demand, flexibility of all resources is required; this applies in particular to labour. Cross-training of the workforce is one mechanism often used.
- *Organisation in modules or cells*. Many JIT factories are organised in small autonomous modules or cells, each cell being totally responsible for its own production and supply of the adjacent module. Within the cell, the workforce is trained to work as a group, and often many activities normally considered as staff functions, such as scheduling and maintenance, are brought into the cell or module.

- *Continuous improvement.* JIT implementation is not a one-off effort; it embodies the ethic of continuous improvement, which needs to be supported by all levels of staff in the production team.
- *JIT purchasing.* Materials and components are purchased in compliance with well-defined requirements in terms of quantity, quality and delivery. The success and resulting performance reliability of this system is based upon co-operation between the purchaser and supplier. This approach ensures that the right quantities are purchased and made at the right time and quality, and that there is no waste.

Two views of JIT prevail. The narrow view sees it as a collection of shopfloor-based techniques concerned with continuous flow management. The broader view – and the one we are concerned with in this book – sees it as continuous flow throughout the entire supply chain, from purchasing to delivery of finished goods and after-sales service, together with all the functions that support efficient production. This is the view that predominates in Japan and, increasingly, in Western manufacturing companies.

Just-in-time is not a single technique. It is more appropriately a philosophy of manufacturing, in which a variety of techniques – approximately 100 have been identified – support the objective of waste-free production to meet known orders. Some of these techniques are well-known in the West – and indeed many originated in Europe or the United States. The manner in which they are combined will vary according to the kind of product, market or base manufacturing technology, but all JIT approaches tend to involve four fundamental areas of activity. These are as follows.

Manufacturing techniques

These are the techniques with which most companies will probably begin their JIT effort. JIT focuses on flow through the operation, and cellular manufacturing is one of the core techniques that leads to flow. A key analytical technique leading to cellular manufacturing is group technology. These are supported by set-up time reduction, a key technique that enables manufacture to be in very small batch sizes. Small batch sizes in turn make continuous flow easier to attain. Once these have been implemented, the next technique that can be used is pull scheduling. This is normally known as Kanban, named after the Japanese for the cards that are often used in this system. There are two forms of Kanban, one-card and two-card. These core techniques are supported by a host of other non-core JIT techniques, such as use of the smallest possible machine, the principles of 'Seiri' (putting away everything that is not needed), 'Seiton' (arranging those things in the best possible way), preventive maintenance, 'Pokayoke' (foolproof devices to prevent mistakes and defects), 'Nagara' (selfdeveloped machines), 'Jidoka' (stopping of the production equipment, automatically or by the worker, when abnormal conditions are sensed or occur), U-shaped lines (within a cell), and standardised packaging and containers.

Production materials control

Manufacturing planning and control systems require adaptation to a JIT environment. Materials requirements planning (MRP) and JIT can mutually support each other, but major adaptations must be made. One common adaptation is 'flat' bills of material, that is bills of material that are simplified to reflect manufacturing as a continuous process rather than a series of independent processes. Another is backflushing. This is a process in which inventory levels are calculated, not by conventional means, but by measuring the daily output and scrap of finished products. From these measurements, management calculates the amount of material that was used that day. This is a simpler system than MRP, because it requires no booking out of stock. It does, however, require the very short process cycle times that come from using JIT.

JIT is greatly helped by reduction of variability, through smoothing of production schedules, via 'optimised production technology' (OPT), and techniques of balancing production ('Heijunka'). Other useful techniques include under-capacity scheduling (deliberately scheduling slack time during each shift so as to allow for problem rectification), and visible production control (minimising control paperwork).

JIT purchasing

This is the aspect of JIT most readily recognised – ensuring that components and materials are supplied in small quantities, in exact months, at frequent intervals and at 100% quality. Naive observers have often noticed the benefits of this approach without recognising that it can only happen as a result of radical change and efficiency improvement within the production environment. Delivering just in time to a factory which is not already operating internally in a JIT manner is likely to exacerbate rather than solve problems. Specific techniques related to JIT purchasing include single sourcing, or more commonly, reducing suppliers to a small number of reliable partners within special relationships, use of standardised containers, supplier certification, point-of-use delivery, supplier controlled pick-up, purchasing Kanban, early supplier involvement in product development, linked information systems, family of parts sourcing, and above all, mutual trust.

Organising for change

Creating an environment where JIT can take root is an essential first step. In Japan, JIT was a natural follow-on from years of investment in quality management. JIT cannot succeed without a parallel and continuous quality programme that emphasises continuous improvement, elimination of waste and simplification of production methods. An important part of quality management practice are on-the-spot, obligatory problem solving techniques and procedures. These are equally essential for effective JIT.

Why is JIT not used by everyone?

Two main barriers appear to prevent companies from taking advantage of JIT. The first is a matter of determination and commitment at top level. JIT requires a fundamental reappraisal of manufacturing practice within the organisation; it invariably involves a great deal of upheaval in manufacturing processes; and it affects not just the production floor, but all the support systems, from order taking and scheduling to goods delivery. For all these reasons, many companies are content to tinker with the existing manufacturing environment, hoping to reap the rewards of greater efficiency without expending the efforts. It rarely succeeds.

The second barrier consists of a host of damaging misconceptions and excuses. Among them:

● MRP is an adequate substitute for JIT, more suitable to Western firms. *Not true.* The two are not exclusive. MRP is much more limited in terms of impact on operational efficiency and bottom line; its implementation is far less costly and disruptive when JIT principles are already practised.
● JIT only works in line high-volume batch production in industries such as electronics. *Not true.* JIT has been successfully applied in industries such as:
  ● Pharmaceuticals.
  ● Paint manufacture.
  ● Whisky bottling.
  ● Distribution.
● JIT requires daily deliveries by suppliers (and mine will not do that). *Not true.* Daily deliveries are an outcome of successful application of JIT within the manufacturing organisation. Only when the company has its own manufacturing processes working in a JIT manner can it draw the full benefits from daily deliveries. At that stage it is able to help suppliers implement similar systems, to mutual advantage.
● We can avoid late delivery to our customers by scheduling

production cycles longer than we absolutely need. *True, but* the extra cost of holding inventory will have a significant effect on overall costs. This is really no more than an unwillingness to accept the discipline that JIT's tight schedules demand. Reductions of 90% in the production cycle are commonplace in companies that have grasped this particular nettle.

● We are a low-volume operation, which will not benefit from JIT. *Not true*, says manufacturing expert Richard Walleigh of management consultants Arthur Young. He explains:

Most production operations involve low volumes. The principles of JIT are just as applicable here as in high-volume operations. Emphasis on reducing setup times, building products in smaller batches, and making things only on demand will improve a small operation as much as a large one.

In fact, a small-volume operation may find it easier to convert to JIT because it may already be making products in small batches using simple equipment with short setup times.

Hewlett-Packard's computer systems division, which builds fewer than six computers a day, has realised tremendous benefits from JIT. These are, however, complex machines with many subassemblies and thousands of individual parts.

● We are doing pretty well already. We are already the cost leader in our sector. *Possibly so*, but for how long? This kind of dangerous complacency leads to problem avoidance. No manufacturing company retains an international cost advantage without constant investment in staying ahead of (or at least keeping pace with) the technology. One of the keys to technology leadership is awareness of where the problems lie. It is also one of the most difficult things to do. JIT's value lies not just in the operational and cost improvements it brings, but in the hidden problems it exposes and forces the organisation to tackle. In the traditional manufacturing environment, by contrast, problems tend to be ignored unless they are obviously hurting.

● JIT will cure all my production headaches. *Not true*. Production problems arise from a whole variety of causes, some of which (for example, payment systems) are not within the control of JIT techniques. A naive belief in the efficacy of JIT can lead to failed implementations, which make it more difficult to gain backing for realistic JIT projects elsewhere in the organisation. It is important to understand what JIT can practically deliver, before embarking on introductory projects. Equally, it is important to begin with projects that are readily implementable and will show clear short-term results.

The way ahead

The Japanese have thrown down the gauntlet in developing new ways of manufacturing and turning these into a new form of competition. This book first looks in more detail at what the Japanese are doing in Japan. It then looks at how JIT has been transferred to the West, with individual chapters on the USA, UK and continental Europe. Each of these chapters contains many short case examples showing the application of JIT in a wide range of industries and environments. The final chapter draws on the lessons of these companies and looks at the ways in which companies can effectively implement JIT.

The challenge of time-based competition

Most industries today, says Joseph D. Blackburn, professor of management at the Owen Graduate School of Management, Vanderbilt University, are vulnerable to the competitor who can use time, or speed of response, as a weapon. In the average manufacturing firm, of the total time required to produce a product and deliver it to the customer, actual work is being performed on the product less than 5% of the time. There are enormous market opportunities to be seized by the firm that can be more time productive and these efforts are underway in many industries.

Time is displacing cost as a critical dimension of competition. The JIT revolution in manufacturing was perhaps the first manifestation of this new type of competition. Through hindsight, the view is emerging that JIT is not an end in itself for a firm, but an evolutionary step toward a longer-term goal of becoming a time-based competitor. The essence of a successful JIT system is time compression; zero inventory and proximity to suppliers, while important, supply only a small portion of the bottomline benefits. The real benefits – the ones that provide a sustainable competitive advantage – are created by a shrinkage in the time required for product to move through the factory. This time compression translates into faster asset turnover, increased output, and flexibility and speed of response to customers. Viewed in this way, diminished inventory is seen as more of a side benefit than a driving force.

Competitively, time compression can provide a manufacturer with a powerful strategic advantage. For instance, consider the introduction of a new product. How long does it take to design and engineer the product and get it into volume manufacturing? Some of the best Japanese firms in the product development area, Honda and Sony for example, can introduce products twice as fast as their Western counterparts, with half the staff. Coupled with a flexible, JIT manufacturing system, these firms can hose the competition with an array of new products and, at the same time, have costs no higher than their slower competitor. The market advantages can be overwhelming.

2. JIT in Japan

Japan is the home of JIT. The basic techniques were developed (and still are being developed) there. In this chapter we look at how JIT came about, the core philosophy of waste reduction, and the variety of approaches Japanese companies have taken to adapting JIT to a variety of circumstances. We also examine Japanese perceptions of JIT as part of manufacturing strategy and examine likely future trends.

2 JIT in Japan

History of JIT

Exactly how JIT emerged as an approach to manufacturing management is obscured in an inevitable cloud of mythology. But it is clear that its development was primarily in Japan and, in particular, in that country's espousal of total quality as the basis of its manufacturing development. The familiarity with problem-solving techniques at all levels in Japanese companies and the constant efforts to simplify and subsequently automate processes to achieve greater consistency and reliability of production all led to a much deeper understanding of how individual production processes worked, and how they fitted into the production cycle.

Although Toyota was not the first company to use JIT – that honour probably belongs to the shipyards, which wanted to establish firmer control over the delivery of steel plate and fittings – it is widely recognised as the company that has done most to promote and develop the concept, both within Japan and globally. Indeed, in Japan, JIT is more commonly referred to as the Toyota production system. The motivations behind Toyota's development of JIT were clearly strategic. Given the fiercely competitive nature of the automobile business in its domestic market and the prediction that the Yen would appreciate strongly in value, Toyota had to reduce costs and increase customer satisfaction radically. Incremental improvements simply would not provide the volume of sales and profit margins necessary to expand into a global manufacturer. Like all automobile manufacturers, it suffered from three major problems, described by members of its production control department in the following terms:

● *The automotive industry is a typical mass production assembly where each vehicle is assembled from several thousand parts that have undergone numerous processes. Therefore, trouble in any of the processes will have a large overall effect.*

● *There are very many different models with numerous variations and with large fluctuations in the demand of each variation.*

● *Every few years, the vehicles are completely remodelled and there are also often changes at a part level.*
In order to avoid the problems of unbalanced inventory and surplus equipment and workers, we put our efforts into developing a production system which is able to shorten the lead time from the entry of materials to the completion of the vehicle.

The basic concept, as applied and described by Toyota, has twin objectives – 'reduction of cost through elimination of waste' and 'to make full use of the workers' capabilities'. The key principles of cost reduction are as follows.

JIT production. The company describes JIT production as the basic process of minimising the lead time from the entry of materials into the plant to the completion of the vehicle. The key components here are the system of Kanban, which literally means 'coded card', and the insistence that 'all processes produce only the necessary parts at the necessary time and have on hand only the minimum stock necessary to hold the processes together'.

The original Kanban system replaced the production computers that specified daily production quotas for each process in the plant. Among the benefits Toyota claims to have arisen from what might in other circumstances be seen as a backward step technologically, are:

● Reduced costs of information processing, because the data required are all readily visible to everyone who needs them.

● Rapid and precise acquisition of information – for example, about the status of production capacity, operating rate, manpower and so on within any production process.

● Up-to-date scheduling information that takes into account last-minute orders.

● More accurate prediction of production quantities needed in preceding processes.

The Kanban system used two kinds of cards – one to authorise conveyance of components from one process to another; one to order production work to be done on the component within the next process. The conveyance card is needed to collect a component from the preceding process, and can only be obtained by taking it from the container of a component actually being worked on. The production card is removed from the components and becomes a despatch note to authorise production of a replacement, if required.

Withdrawal by subsequent processes. The traditional method of production organisation was – and largely still is – for each process to produce parts according to a preplanned master schedule. Each process is responsible for keeping the following process supplied with enough parts to maintain continuity of production. In practice, this approach makes every downstream process heavily reliant on variables it cannot influence or control; at the same time, it is difficult to insert rapid changes into the system, because it is so complex.

Toyota's system turned this approach on its head, so that production was driven by the withdrawal of parts by the following process, rather than a production plan. In effect, it says that the only process that should determine the necessary timing and quantity of component manufacture and delivery is the final assembly line. Subassembly cells manufacture only to demand and pull their requirements from processes further down the line on exactly the same basis.

One-piece production and conveyance. All processes are re-designed to approach the condition where they can optimally produce a single component for a specific order and convey it singly to the next process as required, with only one piece in the buffer stock between processes. While this represents an ideal that may not always be achievable in practice, it effectively prevents production by lots and hence the accumulation of buffer stocks.

Cutting lot size in this manner involves greatly shortening set-up times; improving production methods to eliminate inventory within processes (e.g. by custom-building multipurpose machining equipment to concentrate on specific families of components); and improving conveyance between processing stations.

Levelling of production. The whole procedure of reliance on pulling components from preceding processes rests upon predictability of demand. If demand is likely to swing by significant amounts, then buffer stocks will tend to be created to cope with peak demand. Here, again in the words of the company's own production control staff, is how Toyota copes with this problem:

> *Just-in-time production makes all processes produce the necessary parts at the necessary time, with only the minimum stock necessary to hold the processes together on hand. In addition, by constantly checking the quantity inventory and production lead times as a matter of policy variables, it shows up the existence of surplus equipment and workers. This is the starting point to the second characteristic of Toyota production system, which is to make full use of the workers' capability.*
>
> *Final assembly lines at Toyota are mixed product lines. Daily production is averaged by taking the number of vehicles in the monthly production schedule as classified in the specifications, and dividing by the number of working days.*
>
> *As regards the production sequence during each day, we calculate the cycle time of each different vehicle specification. To meet the different cycle times, vehicles of differing specification follow each other along the line.*
>
> *If the final assembly line levels the production in this way, then production in all subsequent processes, one-piece production and conveyance are also levelled.*

The second significant point in levelled production is to observe the basic rule of just-in-time; to produce only as much as can be sold. On the one hand we adjust the production level to meet the changes in the market; on the other hand, we produce as smoothly as possible within a certain range. Even after the monthly production schedule has been decided, Toyota will still make changes in the specification of vehicles on the basis of daily orders. Even when we reach capacity, Toyota will make revisions in the monthly schedule to reduce the shock of market fluctuation as much as possible.

This production system can operate with smaller production changes than normal scheduled production systems. Consequently, it will be possible to work with less equipment capacity and a more stable number of workers. (This is specially important to Japanese companies that have lifetime employment systems.)

Jidoka. The term 'Jikoka' as used at Toyota means 'to make the equipment or operation stop whenever an abnormal or defective condition arises'. In short, its distinctive feature lies in the fact that when an equipment problem or machining defect occurs, the equipment or entire line stops. Any line can also be stopped in this way.

Jidoka also refers to the automatic shutdown that occurs when the machine has produced exactly the specified number of components. It will only resume operations when a further order is fed into the production cell or line from the next stage in the production process.

The key principles Toyota identifies under 'making full use of workers' capabilities' are as follows.

Elimination of waste movement. This refers both to the removal of unnecessary handling and materials transportation and to the amount of time spent watching machines. Both of these concepts are explored in more detail later in this chapter. Under this heading, says Toyota, also come operations that are by nature not suitable for workers. These are operations involving danger, operations harmful to health, operations requiring hard physical labour, and monotonous repetitive operations; these have been mechanised, automated and unmanned.

The third waste is workers' movements as a result of problems of defects. Thorough 'Jidoka', Toyota has greatly reduced this kind of waste.

Consideration for workers' safety. Strictly monitored policies outlaw tinkering with machines just to keep them running – rather than stopping them to effect proper repairs and adjustments. This is partly a matter of maintaining consistent product quality, but equally a recognition that most accidents occur when people attempt to take short cuts. Toyota's industrial accident record is about half the average of the US automobile industry.

'Self-display of workers' ability'. By this, Toyota means giving employees a significant degree of control and influence over the running and improvement of their workshops. (It does not, however, mean giving free rein for them to change production methods or machine settings.) Again, as the company itself describes it:

> *All workers at Toyota have a right to stop the line on which they are working.*
> *Even in a long line like the final assembly line, if any abnormality comes up, such as the worker finding himself unable to keep up or discovering an incorrect or defective part, he can stop the entire line by pressing the stop button near at hand. It is not a conveyor that operates men; it is men who operate a conveyor. This is the first step to respect for human independence.*
> *As the second step, at all shops in Toyota, the workers are informed of the priority order of the parts to be processed and the state of production advancement. Therefore, the authority for decisions of job despatching and overtime is delegated to the foreman. This allows each shop to conduct production activities without orders from the control department.*
> *As the third step, Toyota has a system whereby workers can take part in making improvements. Any employee at Toyota has a right to make an improvement on the waste he has found.*
> *In the just-in-time production, all processes and all shops are kept in the state where they have no surplus so that if trouble is left unattended, the line will immediately stop running and will affect the entire plant. The necessity for improvement can be easily understood by anyone.*
> *Therefore, Toyota is endeavouring to make up a working place where not only the managers and foremen but also all workers can detect trouble. This is called 'visible control'.*

Other Japanese companies were quick to recognise the potential of this approach. In copying, they added refinements of their own. Among the first to do so were Toyota's own suppliers, who needed to improve their own efficiency to meet the automobile company's tight delivery schedules.

Many other companies have subsequently adapted the Toyota production system to cope with a wide range of environments. A number of case examples are given throughout this chapter. For example, Fujitsu has adapted it to a high-tech environment. Maxcell has adapted it to a process environment (it calls it 'Maxcell minimum stock system'). One important development is the way a number of Japanese companies – for example, Fujitsu – have adapted JIT so that it works alongside a material requirement planning (MRP) system. Another development is the involvement of maintenance in JIT. New approaches to the role of maintenance have been developed by companies such as Tokai Rubber. These approaches go under the name of total productive maintenance.

Waste elimination – a core philosophy of JIT

The essence of JIT rapidly expanded to become a philosophy of waste reduction rather than techniques to resolve specific problems. One definition describes it as 'a disciplined programme for improving overall productivity and the elimination of waste'. Under this definition, productivity is hampered by various kinds of waste, all of which can be removed or reduced by the use of JIT principles. Waste in the manufacturing environment is seen as being composed of 12 key causes, described by the Japanese as follows.

Waste of tentative placement

How components are handled within the production process. The greater the variety of shape, size and operations, the greater the complexity of handling. JIT manufacturing aims to simplify and standardise operations to make handling as easy as possible.

Idle time

Idle time arises for a host of reasons, most obviously from breakdowns or lack of material or components to process. But the Japanese include in idle time, the time spent by operators watching to ensure that the machine is working properly and that the product is perfect. Machine watchers are dispensed with in favour of sensors and switches that keep an automatic watch over machine operation and product quality. The operators are trained to perform multiple functions and given a whole bank of machines to look after. When the machine runs into a problem it cannot fix itself, it calls the operator, who either fixes it or calls for help. Idle time now becomes a function of machine maintenance rather than a fixed occupation.

For Toyota, the objective is to break the chain between the operator and his machine. The company explains:

In the just-in-time production, even when there is surplus capacity in the equipment, only as much as the subsequent process has withdrawn is produced. Thus, if the equipment and workers are tied together, workers are subject to idleness. To prevent such waste of waiting time being created, various improvements have been made such as (1) separating the workers from the equipment by assigning a worker to multiple equipment, (2) concentrating workers' zones at the automatic lines, and (3) making up lines that do not require supervisory operation.

One of the lessons learned by Nissan in developing JIT was that the critical factor in selecting robot manufacturing systems was not the mean time between breakdowns, but the mean time to repair failures. A machine that is out of commission on average for 30 seconds every hour will have less negative impact upon production flow than one which works perfectly for several months, then requires half a day and a team of engineers to repair it.

Waste of movement

The lines of people so often seen seated at conveyor belts in Western factories are inefficient, say the Japanese, who claim that productivity can be increased by an average of 20%, simply by redesigning work stations so that operators stand up. An almost obsessive attention to ergonomics leads Japanese factories to design work stations that require the minimum of excess movement. Wherever possible, loads are designed to weigh less than 10kg. Above 10kg, they are moved not by forklift truck, but on rollers, so the operator does not need to change his centre of gravity.

Waste of overproduction

JIT aims to produce exactly the amount of product the customers require, and no more. Any excess production – at any place in the production process – ties up cash in inventory and may eventually be written off. The solution is to define the inventory levels required at each stage with great precision and to maintain those levels very strictly. While ideally, the production process should be able to operate with no internal inventory at all, in practice most departments will create a small buffer stock, which has to be stored within their own area. The limitation on storage space helps hold down the amount of inventory that can accumulate, but the strongest control is the requirement to stop production when buffer stocks reach a certain level.

Waste of readjustments, defects and returned goods

This is where JIT impinges most strongly on total quality management. Every reject creates a delay in the extended production system (from order to customer), so quality management is an essential ingredient in maintaining production flow.

Waste of set-up times

Some of the most dramatic improvements in productivity have come from reductions of set-up time. Again, Toyota provides the classic example. To achieve top management's demand for a manufacturing lead time of just 2 days, Toyota's engineers had to reduce the time to reset body-panel presses from a current world-best practice of 4 hours to no more than 12 minutes.

Waste of transportation

Every time a component is moved from one place to another, it creates delays. The solutions lie in improving transportation systems so that components that have to be moved arrive at the next machine in the minimum time possible, and in redesigning both components and manufacturing processes so that more activities can be carried out within the same production cell.

Waste of the process itself

A process may be wasteful; or it may be totally unnecessary and capable of being completely eliminated. The reason it is wasteful may be that it does not add value or because there are alternative, better ways of producing the same results. For example, a heat treatment process may be eliminated by the selection of materials that do not require heat treatment. This focus on the waste of the process is particularly useful when applied to service processes.

Waste of materials or subassemblies

This is undoubtedly one of the major forms of waste in terms of cost. Excess usage of material and poor yields from processes can come from a myriad of causes. These can include improper design or specification, poor supplier quality, inadequate process capability, poor handling and storage, misplacement, shrinkage and theft. To eliminate this form of waste, management must pay attention to quality in all aspects of design, supply and processes.

Waste of rewriting

The paperwork of many companies is complex, demands high levels of effort and is error prone. Toyota and other companies have striven to develop exceptionally simple and robust systems that eliminate the need continually to update and change schedles, or to issue new job tickets with every batch produced. Kanban is such a system. In this system production and purchasing is triggered by a card or signal (Kanban). Changes in production are automatically translated through the system by the Kanban without the need to issue new departmental schedules. Often the only action needed is to increase the number of Kanbans in circulation. Development of simple systems is behind the elimination of the waste of rewriting.

Waste of improper order and arrangement

Tidiness is almost a fetish in Japanese JIT environments. This is not a matter of maintaining appearances. Rather, it is a visible manifestation of an extensive and thorough approach to factory housekeeping.

Waste of miscommunication

Many Japanese companies audit managers on the clarity and accuracy of their communications. They do so because they recognise the problems that can arise when instructions are misunderstood. One common aid is a simple checklist that people can work through before sending off each memo.

The economic background to JIT

JIT in Japan has also been shaped by a very different approach to the finances of manufacturing. Whereas in the West, selling price tends to be fixed by adding production cost and profit, then adjusting for competitive factors, Japanese JIT operations begin with a fixed selling price, from which profit targets are deducted. What is left over then becomes the target production cost, which the engineering department has to achieve (Fig. 2.1). The importance of this apparently simple difference in approach cannot be understated. The Japanese companies fix the target selling price after extensive market research and study of the likely entry costs of expected competitors. Achievement of profit becomes far more reliant on cost reduction (which is in the company's control), than on achieving specific levels of sales (which is less in its control).

One of the implications of this approach to financing capital investment is that unused capacity is no longer a sin. In a choice between investment in stock and investment in machine capacity to allow for peaks of demand, the Japanese companies almost invariably conclude that the equipment costs are lower. Calculations of maximum permitted payback time for installing new equipment are relatively long – typically at least 3.5 years, and sometimes up to 5 years.

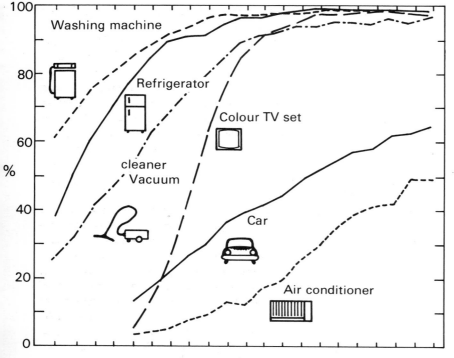

Fig. 2.1 Transition of ownership ratios of consumer durables in Japan. (Source: Economic Planning Agency, Japan)

Over the past decade, the driving force behind JIT has changed substantially, largely as a result of internal pressures within the Japanese domestic economy, which is one of the most competitive – arguably *the* most highly competitive – in the world. Prof. H. Yamashina, one of the principal exponents of JIT in Japan, explains that the major domestic competitive pressures now include:*

● *A high degree of market saturation in many sectors Out of Japanese consumers, 180% own a colour television. Virtually every major consumer goods product has to operate in a heavily saturated market. Japanese companies create continued demand by reinforcing consumers' natural suspicion of anything second-hand (used cars have far lower value than anywhere else in the developed world) and by obsessive segmentation.*

Marketing of consumer durables concentrates on finding and exploiting minutely different needs. To persuade the householder with one air conditioner that he needs more, the manufacturers produce a wide range that will allow each room to have a conditioner that matches its decor or function. Casio, for example, has dozens upon dozens of different designs of calculator, each aimed at a narrow market segment

A number of well-documented cases indicate that size of market share correlates directly with the number of production variations,

*Reproduced by permission from *Strategic Direction*, 5 Bridge Avenue, Maidenhead, Berks, SL6 1RR.

says Yamashina. He quotes the case of Honda, which was forced into a motorcycle price war by Yamaha. Honda's defence was not just to match prices, but also to bring out more and more new designs. Yamaha was rapidly pushed into such big losses that it had to pull back.

- *Demand for rapid delivery. All Japanese manufacturers, says Yamashina, now find they have to compete on three fundamentals – price, quality (including service) and delivery date. The latter is so important that one shoe manufacturer has installed a laser-measurement system in retail outlets, where customers can choose a style then have the exact fitting taking for their feet. The information is relayed to the factory overnight and and the shoes made up the following day for direct delivery.*

- *Difficulty in forecasting customer demand. Japanese consumers are increasingly fashion conscious. The primary response by producers has been to invest more and more in market research and the creation of extensive feedback systems to relay market information to production and product design as rapidly as possible. Key sources of information are customer surveys and complaints. One major housebuilder completely redesigns his product range every year, to take account of customer research.*

- *Shorter product life cycles. As in other developed countries, the lifetime of new products is constantly reducing. The prime example is the personal computer (PC), which now has a 4–6 month product lifetime in Japan.*

The practice of JIT in Japan

There is no such thing as a typical JIT programme in Japan. Nevertheless, in almost all cases, the core of JIT consists of three parts – flow, flexibility and developing the chain of supply. Japanese factories are characterised by great concern for developing flow in manufacture. The contributors to flow include layout, material handling, cellular manufacture, group technology, a focus on the process, balance and the use of multiple small machines rather than one large one. Flow is supported by flexibility. Much has been written about the use of flexible automation, and certainly many Japanese companies use it to support JIT. However, recent studies by the University of Warwick indicate that flexibility is also gained by use of very small batches (made possible by reduced set-up or changeover times), flexibility in the work force and spare physical capacity. Japanese companies also emphasise developing the chain of supply. This includes getting suppliers to deliver to the point of use, frequent delivery by suppliers in small lots at precise times and giving excellent data to suppliers to allow them to do this. At the customer end, this includes 'making today what is needed tomorrow' and rate-based production scheduling.

Closely associated with this is the great attention paid to developing good forecasts and production plans. What in Western terminology is called the 'master production schedule', is prepared very carefully and used to 'drive' JIT manufacturing. Master production schedules invariably have a period of 10 days in which there is stability. Finally, the core of JIT is developed in most companies in a clear strategic context. Many companies, when talking about their JIT practices, preface them with a statement of corporate and market strategy and how these practices fit in with the strategy. Let us look at these in more detail.

Continuous flow

'The Japanese make absolutely no concessions when it comes to the production flow; goods must flow' (K. van Eynde, manager, logistics support, DAF Trucks).

Every time the line stops, it is unproductive. The traditional Western response to this problem has been to design dedicated plants that produce long runs of products with minimal variations. Downtime usually occurs through breakdown or shortage of materials. JIT, on the other hand, assumes that production runs will be short and starts from a basis of minimising downtime at the setting-up stage. It therefore concentrates on improving production flow through the following.

Layout
Layouts are designed so as to locate sequential operations both one after the other and close together so as to maximise flow, minimise travel and to simplify material handling (Fig. 2.2).

Fig. 2.2 Casing line at Mitsubishi Heavy Industries plant in Kyoto

Materials handling

Well-designed materials handling can help promote a smooth flow of goods and minimise damage through handling. Japanese companies often use a combination of the very simple (gravity feed rather than conveyors) and the sophisticated (automated guided vehicles: AGVs).

Cells

The use of cellular manufacture, where a set of products manufactured in a small cell greatly reduces the distance travelled by the product or component.

Group technology

This is a structured approach to identifying groups of parts with similar manufacturing characteristics. If a group of parts can be found, then a cellular manufacturing approach can be used.

Focus on the process

In the West, the first group of people to examine JIT in detail were those in production control. They focused on the planning and control elements such as Kanban, and saw JIT as a production control tool. This is a major misconception. In Japan JIT focuses on the process; designing and managing the process for high-quality, closely coupled, small-batch and reliable manufacture.

Flexibility

Flexibility in Japanese companies comes from the following four sources.

Small batches

One of the key elements of JIT is manufacturing in small batches – manufacturing today that which is needed tomorrow. Small-batch manufacturing will minimise work in process inventory, reduce lead time and produce much greater flexibility in manufacture. One of the main techniques leading to small-batch manufacture is set-up time reduction.

Spare capacity

Even under conditions of stable demand, customer mix in Japan is subject to great fluctuation. A very common approach in Japan is to have some spare physical capacity. This allows companies to respond rapidly to customer and market changes by switching manufacture and the workforce from one set of capacity to another.

Flexible labour

Japanese factories are characterised by having extremely flexible labour. This flexibility comes through high levels of cross-training, and through the willingness of labour to transfer from one job to another.

Flexible automation
There is wide use of flexible automation in Japanese factories, sometimes simple, sometimes very sophisticated. This is a major contributor to the flexibility of JIT.

The chain of supply

Point-of-use supply
Many Japanese JIT factories are designed to allow delivery to any point round the outside. In many industries the parts are delivered to the point in the production process where they will be used, so eliminating the need for intermediate storage or handling.

Frequent delivery
Delivery from suppliers, particularly a high-volume manufacturer, is regular – as many as 6–10 deliveries per day of a part.

Data to suppliers
Suppliers cannot make frequent deliveries in small lots unless they have an excellent forecast and forward schedules from their customers. Japanese companies pay particular attention to giving robust forward schedules to suppliers, often with the use of electronic data interchange.

Make today what is needed tomorrow
The essence of JIT as practised in Japan is to couple the assembly of products tightly to the market demand, and to couple the manufacture of sub-assemblies and parts tightly to the final assembly.

Rate-based production
Many companies practising JIT are scheduled on the basis of a fixed rate of production per day, rather than on the basis of orders received. This is often accompanied by visible signals indicating cumulative production versus target. With rate-based production, the production rates of feeder departments and of suppliers can be matched to the final assembly rate.

Driving these core activities is a production forecast and plan, both of which derive in turn from a clear and detailed vision of the market in the short and medium terms. This vision of the future is much more than a paper exercise; it becomes the guideline for investment in future productivity increases and may assume a steady or lower selling price for the product at increased profit levels. It therefore places great pressure upon managers to achieve significant cost and productivity breakthroughs. Managers in Japanese companies are left in no doubt that JIT is seen by top management as a strategic issue. When these companies talk about their JIT practices, they usually preface their remarks with a statement of corporate and market strategies, and how JIT practices fit within those strategies.

The core activities of JIT are in turn supported by a range of management tools, techniques and top management commitments, as illustrated in Fig. 2.3. These are explained in greater detail in Chapter 6, which discusses the effective implementation of a JIT programme. In brief, however, the primary tools are:

● *Housekeeping*. When discussing manufacturing in Japan, one is always struck by the numerous philosophies or sets of principles widely quoted. One such set is good 'housekeeping', which seems

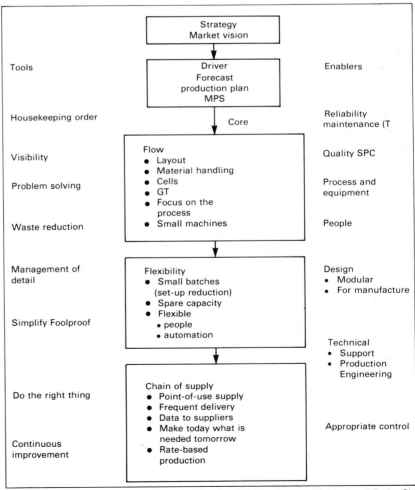

Fig. 2.3 Japanese JIT manufacturing management practices

*Reproduced by permission from *Strategic Direction*, 5 Bridge Avenue, Maidenhead, Berks, SL6 1RR.

to be universal in Japan. It is summarised by the four 'S's: Seiri (orderliness), Seiton (tidiness), Seiso (clarity), and Seiketsu (cleanliness). The application of these is an important and widely used tool.

- *Visibility*. There are a number of JIT techniques associated with making production visible which are widely used in Japan. These include the use of 'Andon' boards (light systems signalling trouble spots), use of containers with special inserts so that quantities can be easily ascertained, and the display of daily operating achievement on TV screens.
- *Problem solving*. Problem solving plays a key role in making JIT happen. First, there is wide training in problem-solving skills. Second, there is an emphasis on solving a problem both immediately and, through determining its root cause, permanently. In addition, forced problem solving is often used. This is the deliberate removal of buffers to bring problems to the surface.
- *Waste reduction*. Another 'philosophy' widespread in Japan is that of the removal of waste. It is summarised by the three 'M's: Muri (unreasonableness), Mura (unevenness) and Muda (waste) – see the box. JIT is supported by the active pursuit of the removal of all sources of waste such as inventory, excess movement and unnecessary activities such as inspection.

Muda, Mura, Muri (3-MU)

The term '3-MU' originates from three Japanese words beginning with the letters MU – *Muda, Mura* and *Muri. Muda* can be literally translated as 'waste, useless or excess'; *Mura* as 'irregular, uneven, or inconsisten'; and *Muri* as 'unreasonable, excessive, or strain'.

Speaking more concretely, *Muda* means a state of things in which materials, equipment or manpower add wasteful cost and contribute nothing to 'add value'. Excess production (over the customers' purchase order), unnecessary processes, downtime, unnecessary movements of workers, excessive inventory, poor-quality products, and moving of materials can all be looked upon as *Muda*.

Mura, which means 'irregular, uneven or inconsistent', occurs where people's work lacks consistency, or materials are delivered intermittently to disturb the smooth constant flow of production. A large volume of work assigned to one person, while others are under-occupied can also be called *Mura*.

Muri means unreasonable, excessive or strained performance that often follows *Muda* and *Mura*. Unreasonably excessive work, which keeps the person unusually busy and gives him no time to inspect the condition of equipment and the quality of products can be regarded as *Muri*.

- *Management of detail*. Japanese firms are characterised by attention by management to detail, and to making sure that the detail is managed.
- *Simplifying and foolproofing*. These are two tools that support the development of flow.
- *Continuous improvement*. Japanese firms seem to have an explicit philosophy that anything that they are doing can be improved further.

Making JIT happen

Flow and flexibility in manufacturing is only possible if much of the uncertainty is taken out and appropriate manpower and technological resources are made available. A striking aspect of JIT as practised by Japanese companies is the extent to which they make sure that steps have been taken to enable JIT to occur. Some of the major steps widely used in Japan include the following:

- *Preventive maintenance*. This is necessary to develop high reliability in machines so as to remove the need for buffering against machine breakdown. Many Japanese companies use 'total productive maintenance'. In this practice, routine maintenance is moved more to the operator and the maintenance function's role becomes one of planning maintenance, major repairs, ensuring that new machines are fully debugged, and training operators.
- *Quality*. The Japanese emphasis on quality and techniques, such as statistical process control, is already well known. Quality management is a key mechanism in making JIT possible. Poor quality in production or in parts supplied makes the application of JIT difficult.
- *Process and equipment*. JIT in Japan is not always built on heavy automation, but on having appropriate, properly used plant and equipment.
- *People*. Japanese companies emphasise the importance of people in making JIT possible. Some of the people components include teamwork, education, particularly of supervisors but also of the operator, flexibility in work practices and in skills, simple payment schemes, appropriate skill levels, and management who understand production.
- *Design*. This has a surprisingly high importance in JIT. First, design for manufacture reduces much of the uncertainty in manufacture. Second, the wide use of modular design makes it possible to produce a very high variety of finished product whilst maintaining simplicity in manufacture. These two together contribute to flow manufacture and flexibility whilst maximising responsiveness to customer needs.
- *Technical support*. Developing flow and flexibility, and supporting it with good equipment, requires a high level of technical support and

good production engineering. The Japanese companies studied by the Warwick researchers are notable for the extent of this support and the excellence of the production engineering.

● *Managerial control*. Many Japanese companies accompany the development of JIT with targets set by management and directly related to the objectives of JIT and long-term control against those targets. Typical managerial control measures include the number of machine breakdowns per month, stock levels, and quality achievement.

Not all Japanese companies are the same

It is important to stress again that the JIT elements chosen will vary considerably between companies. There is no single set pattern of JIT, no more than there is a single recipe for effective manufacturing.

As we have already discussed in Chapter 1, misconceptions about the nature of JIT are common amongst Western firms. Generalisations based upon a few companies, such as Toyota, do not necessarily represent the reality in the majority of successful Japanese manufacturing firms. These misconceptions extend to the tools and enabling systems as much as to the JIT process itself. The fact is that the Japanese companies themselves have a wide diversity of opinion and practice concerning many of these elements of JIT. Take, for example, the techniques of Kanban, quality circles, single source purchasing, automation and zero inventory. Kanban is still only used by a relatively small number of companies in Japan, most of which are characterised by low complexity of both production process and product. Some companies reject Kanban outright. For example, the production director of Hitachi claims 'We do not use Kanban. It is too harsh.'

Quality circles have expanded remarkably in Japan and are one of the most widely transferred techniques. The Japanese Union of Scientists and Engineers has a paid circulation of more than 200 000 for its monthly quality magazine. But not every company welcomes them and some regard them as frankly dysfunctional. Says one Japanese manager: 'Many Japanese companies have not achieved everything they have expected from quality circles. At the start, members are only motivated by incentives. I want *everyone* aware that quality is everyone's problem. Each individual must be responsible for quality. Quality circles do not promote this awareness. Only after this awareness and understanding is present could quality circles be of use.' Another Japanese manager explains that quality circles are concerned with solving problems long after they occur. He requires his workforce to solve problems immediately, not to wait to discuss them.

Single-sourcing of components is largely a myth. While many companies single-source some suppliers, most Japanese manufacturers aim at least to dual-source and often have specific policies outlining the proportion of product that should be allocated to primary and secondary suppliers. Single-sourcing usually occurs where the supplier would have to make a major investment in tooling, or where both supplier and purchaser engage in a joint development effort. Outside Japan, Japanese companies may also single-source when they simply cannot find more than one reliable supplier – as is often the case.

While Japanese companies frequently do have a major investment in automation, JIT does not appear to be dependent on massive investments in robotics and other advanced manufacturing. Indeed, one British subsidiary of a Japanese company is achieving similar improvements in productivity through JIT from plants where there have been major investments in capital equipment and plants where there have been virtually none. The divergence of attitudes towards automation amongst Japanese manufacturers is illustrated by these two statements:

> *If a worker is involved in the production line, then there is the possibility of a fault. If production is automated and the machine is well-maintained, then the product will be more reliable. I strongly request production engineers to make no workers involved in the production line (General Manager, Tokai Works, Hitachi).*

> *When we make modifications or improvements to a process, we do not want completely automated machinery. Because of the 'respect for human systems' point of view, automation can be counteractive. The important thing is to let people feel that they are responsible and take pride in their responsibility and in their achievements. There are cases where full automation is essential, but as a whole people are more important than automation (Production Director, Sumitomo).*

Similarly, views on how far to go in removing buffer stocks vary considerably from company to company. While some aim to remove all inventory from the system, others take a more relaxed view and even have specific policies for buffer inventories.

Is Japanese culture necessary for JIT?

Western manufacturers observing JIT often see only the existing processes, rather than the multiple, painstaking steps that have preceded them. They often remark also on the culture that supports 'the Japanese work ethic' – usually to bemoan the inadequacies of their own shopfloor workers. But the cultural difference is, in the main, a red herring. In reality, responsiveness of the workers lies in the following four areas.

Training

For many Japanese companies training is a strategic issue, administered by a senior executive. Its objectives are clear. Among them:

- To allow rapid transfer of workers from one task to another, without loss of efficiency.
- To provide a broader job perspective, so people can place each task in context.
- To allow the worker to play an active part in problem prevention and problem solving.
- To speed the movement of pilot lines into the regular, fault-free production.

Japanese engineering recruits are typically subjected to up to 2 years' intensive training, moving around the factory, to learn in detail how it works. Ordinary shopfloor workers also receive a great deal of training, both in their induction period and as part of the regular routine of work.

Individual decision making

Many Western observers assume that the mores of Japanese society, where achieving consensus is important and where individualism is not encouraged, is automatically carried into the workplace. While this is true to some extent, it does not mean that the individual worker has constantly to seek permission to make changes to work procedures. In practice, he usually has a much greater freedom to make on the spot decisions than his Western counterpart. This is partly because his more extensive training gives him the know-how to be trusted with engineering decisions, but also because the systems are designed to allow interventions that meet key criteria – for example, stopping the line to assess and remedy a quality fault.

More engineers

Fig. 2.4 illustrates the typical composition of a large Western factory and its Japanese counterpart. Japanese manufacturing companies tend to have fewer operators and more engineers than their Western counterparts. The engineers concentrate on design and redesign of product and production processes for simplicity of manufacture; and on preventing breakdowns. Unlike their Western counterparts they tend not to be functional specialists. Each has a substantial knowledge in all the functions of quality control, industrial

Fig. 2.4 Production techniques of four levels. (Source: Prof. H. Yamashina, Kyoto University, Japan)

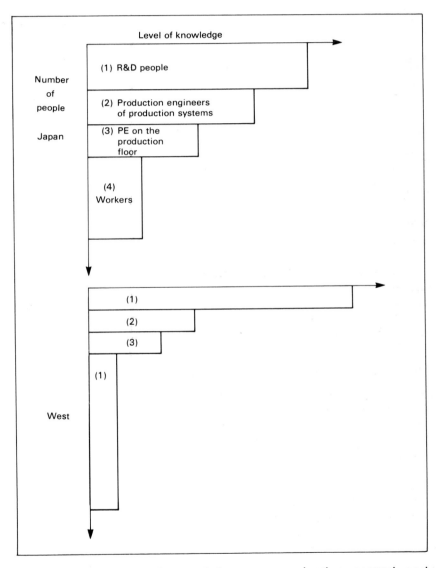

engineering, preventative maintenance, production control and production development. This broad knowledge enables them to design their own new production equipment, customised exactly to their production needs – an option which very few Western companies would normally consider.

The point is supported by Ray Jewitt of management consultants A.T. Kearney, who says:

We hear a lot about indirect/direct ratios in the UK as a key measure. Certainly the Japanese I spoke to were not interested in such ratios. They were concerned with transferring direct labour

from the factory floor to the engineering and quality departments.
In each company I visited, there were substantial numbers of staff
in the engineering departments, development design and product
engineering.

Motivation

Japanese companies tend to spend a great deal of time and effort
sustaining people's motivation to make JIT and associated processes
such as total quality management work. Apart from training, which
increases in periods of recession, partly as a means of keeping active
employees who cannot be laid off, and partly as an investment aimed
at achieving faster growth than the competition as the recession
eases:

● They make extensive use of slogans and campaigns, through
   which top management communicates current priorities for
   improvements. Over and above these are broader slogans of
   corporate purpose. For example:
●   Sharp: 'There is always something to improve and extend. That is
   the reason for being.'
●   Seiko: 'The harmonious relationship of man to machine and man
   to fellow man makes reliability in our products and excellence in
   our technology.'
●   Nissan: 'Customer satisfaction will lead to a larger market share.'
The value of these slogans, which can easily be dismissed by Western
observers as window dressing, lies less in their sentiment than in the
very real commitment to them that top management demonstrates.
● They are prepared to share the benefits of increased productivity
   with the employees. An example quoted by Prof. Yamashina is the
   renovation of a bottling plant by beverages company Suntory. The
   old bottling line that required 75 people to operate was replaced by
   a highly automated JIT system that required 20 people who handle
   multiple machines, do their own maintenance and run the master
   computer. The operators shared in the savings.
Certainly, the Japanese do not see themselves as having an
especially strict work ethic. The basic working hours for production
workers are not very different from those in the West, at about 2000 a
year. The president of Hyundai, the Korean manufacturing con-
glomerate, recently described Japanese workers as lazy by comparison with Koreans, who work 3000 hours a year. Nonetheless, up to 2
hours' overtime per day is quite common in Japanese factories, as a
means of coping with extra demand. Once this safety net is broken
through, companies operating JIT tend to have networks of part-
timers and subcontractors to fall back upon. The limiting factor in
coping with sudden peaks of demand is machine capacity. Here,
however, Japanese companies using JIT are often better placed than

their Western counterparts, because as we have observed above, their production flows are designed to run much of their equipment below capacity.

Japanese manufacturing strategy – automation and JIT in partnership

Ray Jewitt, of management consultants A.T. Kearney, recently visited Japan on an IFS study tour, to compare JIT progress in Europe and Japan. Among his most significant observations are the following.

Manufacturing strategy

The Japanese appear to have a national manufacturing strategy, although they do not discuss it. It is based on a few important precepts, the two main ones being:

● All markets will eventually become saturated.
● The customer is the objective.

So how do the Japanese translate that view of the future into manufacturing requirements? What sets a manufacturer or company above the rest? The answer is, the ability to introduce new products rapidly, efficiently and reliably. Hence manufacturing processes and systems are designed to that end. The focus is, therefore, on how manufacturing will contribute to increasing and varied customer demands.

For example, one of the companies I visited was called Omron. This company manufactures a whole range of products from relays to vending machines, automatic cash dispensers, cash registers, traffic control systems, and optical control systems. It sees a conflict between diversification and standardisation. Its response to this conflict was to develop a flexible manufacturing system (FMS). By this it did not mean a FMS as it is recognised in the UK (i.e. a cell of automated machines producing a product or a group of products). Omron meant the whole factory. Fig. 2.5 shows how Omron views its migration path to where it is today. It starts with mixed production, concentrating on set-up changeovers and flexibility of the process route through to diversify production, concentrating on retrofitting machines, moving on to synchronise production linking machines and finally, to totally automated production.

The statement 'The customer is the objective' is extremely important, in that the Japanese customer is the objective in manufacturing, not computerintegrated manufacture (CIM) or advanced manufacturing technology (AMT).

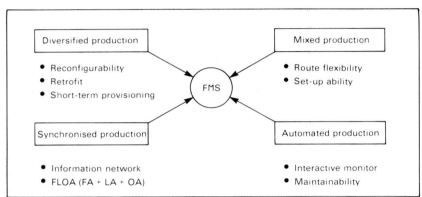

Applying automation

Fig. 2.6 shows Nippondenso's progress through the automation route, starting with what it calls spot or point automation, through line automation, through area automation, through to what it describes as cube or solid automation. In its particular strategy, it defines its requirements in this way: diversified products plus high productivity equals a factory automation production system.

It set itself targets on its automation line for radiator production. It did a considerable amount of size, cycle-time and changeover analysis. It analysed designs, with one of its designers permanently working at Toyota. It looked to the future requirements of radiators and found that it could produce what it calls three-core assemblies of radiator, which could in turn result in many diversified types of radiator. It then set about an automation programme which took 3 years from conception through to full implementation and operation. The targets it set during this project were in the following areas:

● *Productivity enhancements*. An improvement of sales per employee by a factor of two, and a reduction in floor space by a factor of

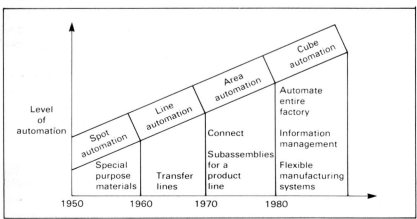

Fig. 2.6 Migration to automation

two. It actually achieved an increase in sales per employee ratio of 2.6 and reduced the floor space by a factor of 2.5.

● *Flexibility*. The achievement of a minimum lot size of 20 units per lot on this particular automation line. It actually achieved 10 units per lot.

● *Quality*. An improvement in quality of 50%. It has achieved an improvement of a third so far.

● *Working environment*. A clean working environment. It has achieved that requirement.

The automation lines are connected to the host computer through fibre-optic local area networks. Automatic bar-coding devices on the lines give them an immediate update of issues and receipts on stock. It is currently linking the host computer to a central computer to make the scheduling operation completely automatic.

Nippondenso tried to design all the equipment and machines itself. This is a common feature of large Japanese companies. In the UK, this is not as straightforward or easy. In many cases companies have to seek external advice, and they should take time now to find companies that can provide them with that sort of capability.

Nippondenso refers to its approach as 'practice policy', which involves:

● Planning quickly and putting into practice quickly.

● Looking at the whole production operation from the view of time, minimising turnaround time.

The Nippondenso approach is well illustrated by the experience of its Nagoya plant. This flexible automated plant supplies radiators and oil coolers to Toyota and other vehicle manufacturers. It was designed to meet demands for varied small lots, while retaining a minimum of work in progress and inventory.

The radiator assembly line is fully automatic and manufactures radiators in batches of 10–100 off. It achieves flexibility through ingenious tooling that enables set-ups to be changed in seconds. It takes in raw material in the form of rolls at one end of the line, and produces assembled, fully tested, and painted radiators at the other end.

Flexible manufacturing systems do not usually allow for small-lot flow and frequent deliveries. The key here is the customer-order Kanban system which triggers shipment from the warehouse. Stock movement in the warehouse triggers the internal Kanban system, whose computer then calculates the optimum product mix, and prints the internal Kanbans for piece part manufacture and assembly. The computer then produces a balanced production schedule every 2 hours. The work is tracked through the plant by automatic reading of the bar codes on the units. Rejects and reworking are also automatically reported. The computer is updated 140 times per day, so the status of the line and programme is instantaneously available. Urgent exceptional orders received by telephone can also be dealt with. They are first fed into the computer, to check the stock. Then an express Kanban is created, the order scheduled into the production programme and the deliveries confirmed with the customer within minutes of receipt.

The line produces 100 000 radiators per month (one every 9 seconds), of 64 types produced at random. The average lead time is 2.5 hours. Toyota receives 24 deliveries per day out of a warehouse that carries only 12 hours' worth of stock. Line utilisation is 80% on the radiator assembly line, of which 5% is due to changeovers and 15% to problems.

The introduction of the Kanban and computer system together with the innovative tooling has resulted in:

- A reduction of 40% in inventory.
- An improvement of 50% in productivity over traditional flexible manufacturing systems.
- A decrease of 50% in management's workload.

'Nippondenso used to have 20 to 30 days' worth of inventories, from raw material to finished products. This has been reduced to 3 to 5 days by adopting JIT and we have the flexibility to handle revised orders. Productivity has improved because problems are specified' (Hajime Sugiura, manager, production control department, Nippondenso).

The road ahead

Japanese companies are now looking to instil JIT into other processes – in particular new product development. Says *Strategic Direction*:

> *Just when Western companies thought that the soaraway yen was bringing them respite from the assault of Japanese high-quality, low cost manufacture, they are about to be hit by another competitive wave: growing variety and ever faster new product introductions. Already the disturbing signs are visible. Japanese motor firms take a quarter the time of the best Europeans and Americans to develop a new model for market. In the early 1980s Honda made 113 motorcycle model changes in 18 months, in effect turning its product line over twice. Company after company is defying manufacturing laws of gravity by increasing productivity and lowering costs at the same time as broadening its product line. How are they performing this apparent miracle? According to George Stalk, Jr. of the Boston Consulting Group, by concentrating on a new dimension of competition: time.*

Toyota provides another example. By the late 1970s Toyota had streamlined its production system to the point where it could make an auto in less than two days. But to their chagrin, eager engineers found further attempts to reduce cycle time were frustrated by sales and distribution departments which needed up to 26 days to close the sale, process the order and deliver the car to the customer. It actually cost more to sell and distribute the car than to make it. To break the logjam, Toyota merged its separate production and sales companies. It quietly retired the previous sales executives and replaced them with JIT-trained managers from production who rapidly introduced into white collar areas the disciplines that had been so successful in reducing time in manufacturing. Out went the traditional information batches; in came just-in-time information. By 1987, the sales and distribution cycle had been cut to eight days, including manufacture. The next target is to be able to deliver an auto to a customer's specification in six days anywhere in Japan, four days in Tokyo.

Japanese companies are now using similar organisational techniques to gain time in new product development – with spectacular results. In industry after industry, Japanese firms can now introduce new products in one-third or one-quarter the time of Western competitors. The 'secret' is again organisation to produce just-in-time results. The structure of a rapid innovation organisation is the same as that of a fast response factory – small batches, multi-functional teams, local rather than complex central scheduling. As in manufacturing, the effect of using these techniques can cut the requirement for time and people in half. Applying them in both manufacturing and product development allows a Japanese company to introduce four times more product than a traditionally organised company with the same amount of time and people.

Case examples

Mazda Corporation

Mazda Corporation employs 25000 people at its Hiroshima automobile plant, producing 1 million vehicles a year. Using JIT it has reduced stock to just 3 hours' worth at each stage of production. Goods are received into a central store 150 yards long by 50 yards wide and 20 feet high, then fed to the assembly lines by stacker trucks. The body assembly line drives all the subassembly cells, pulling components through only as required. The size of buffer stocks in the subassembly cells is limited by the storage space available. The lines are not dedicated to particular models; each car is effectively custom made, with the specific instructions fed to the computers en route by bar codes on the route card. On the final assembly line, the same principles apply, with a central computer delivering to each work station exactly the right components for that customer's specifications. Again, buffer stocks are minimal – enough to deal with three cars at any work station.

A rolling 6-month schedule is produced at 1-month intervals, with a rolling 1-month schedule at 10-day intervals. Within those schedules, fine tuning to meet customer requirements can take place up to 30 minutes before assembly commences, although 3 hours before is the normal cut-off time. Suppliers receive 3 days' rolling notice of requirements. Delivery is either every 4 hours, every 8 hours or every 16 hours, according to category of component. Variation in demand is accommodated mainly by varying the speed of the line or by overtime.

Mazda's JIT programme has reduced total lead times through the body line, painting and final assembly to a mere 22 hours, meaning that customers can expect to receive vehicles within 2 weeks from receipt of order. The company does hold stock – about 20 days' worth – but this is primarily for export.

Mitsubishi Aluminium

Mitsubishi Aluminium was founded in 1962 by Mitsubishi and Reynolds International Inc. of the USA. The Fuji plant near Tokyo was completed in June 1965 and comprises three main divisions:

- *Sheet rolling*. Up to 2.7 m wide, on a 4-Hi reversible hot mill, various cold mills, a roughing mill and a finishing mill.
- *Extrusion*. The plant is equipped with several hydraulic extrusion presses ranging from 1500 to 3500 tonnes capacity.
- *Foil and packaging*. Foil stock processed through hot and cold mills is fed through foil mills and rolled down to 6 μm thickness.

The company now has 850 employees at Fuji and processes 11 000 tonnes of aluminium products.

Dr H. Nakamura arrived as senior managing director and general manager of the Fuji plant in July 1986. On 1 September, he announced his new initiative for improving competitiveness, which he called the MAF production system. MAF stands for 'Mitsubishi Aluminium Fuji Plant'. It is aimed at three defects affecting production:

- Waste (Muda).
- Irregularity (Mura).
- Excessiveness (Muri).

A steering committee, called the Improvement Project Team, was set up with 23 representatives from the three divisions. Its task was to plan and coordinate MAF. Each division set up its own project team, and other project teams were set up in staff areas like technical control and the cafeteria.

First forty days

Dr Nakamura saw the initial task as one of 'broad slimming'. The attack on waste was focused by the project teams on four areas:

- *Offices*. Streamlining office paperwork was seen as the first choice, because it would be a good example to production. The following instructions were given:
  - No documents must be left on a desk when leaving the office.
  - All field documents must be examined. All unnecessary documents must be weighed and destroyed.
  - Brochures and catalogues which are more than 1 year old must be destroyed.

  Japan Industrial Standards (JIS) required documents to be kept for 5 years, a requirement that was over-ruled. 'We believe that the true objective of the JIT system is to establish an efficient production system rather than excessive completeness of paperwork', said Dr Nakamura.
- *Simplified reports*. An instruction required reports to be summarised on one page. All documents were to be marked with a 'destroy by' date. In this way, a new build-up of documents would be avoided.
- Spare parts. Spare parts and tools were sorted and reorganised to make them easy to see and to access. Dr Nakamura described this as 'putting life into spare parts'.
- Kanban. Mitsubishi Aluminium makes to order because of many combinations of width, length, thickness and alloy specification. It was felt, however, that Kanban cards would be very effective for scheduling the rolling sequence of coils with the hot mill and planning daily production volumes. Details would have to be determined by time units and sequences appropriate to the different processes.

All improvements were to be achieved as early as possible, measured and reported to the workers.

Early results

With typical Japanese drive and energy, the project teams set out their task. Here are some examples of early progress:

- *Cast house*. Over 2000 nuts and bolts were discarded, along with 17 tonnes of bricks and 1.2 tonnes of documents. The heavy steel doors from the tools and parts cabinets were removed (184 pieces). Tools and parts were checked to determine minimum kinds and quantities. All the surplus was scrapped. Because the cast house is dusty, polycarbonate doors were fitted, together with a list of contents for each cabinet.

  Kanban cards were written for each slab held in stock, and were displayed on an inventory board in the workers' rest room where everyone could see it. Kanbans were colour coded for alloy specification and also for age. Red marks meant that the slabs were over 2 months old. For example: within 6 weeks, the publicity thus given to average stock had resulted in a reduction from 1200 to 995 slabs (1230 tonnes).

- *Coil rolling.* Some 3.4 tonnes of paper were discarded, and 9 tonnes of steel material. Stored parts and tools became a structured task, with shadow boards on tool panels used for orderly arrangement.

  Computerised control of coils in process was augmented by Kanban cards. Displayed on an inventory board, the cards again help workers to know the state of coils in progress, and to identify surplus and average coils.

  Hot coils took 2 days to cool off. Cutting this down by one day would save 500 tonnes of inventory. Early attempts at water-cooling the coils resulted in corrosion damage. (The answer was eventually found to be fan-assisted air cooling).

Following this initial phase of restructuring, the shopfloor and walls were painted in ice blue, with dark blue gangways. This helps further to promote cleanliness and tidiness. Set off by mercury vapour lamps and the bright product, the workplace already shows the benefits of MAF.

Dr Nakamura had demonstrated how it was possible to apply the concepts of waste, irregularity and excessiveness to Mitsubishi Aluminium. Already, workers were coming to accept that operating with a smaller stock was better than what they had been doing. Once four simple areas had so far been attacked, he was able to tackle many more.

Among the significant results recorded by Dr Nakamura are:

- Cutting the in-process inventory by half.
- Reducing the lead time by half.
- Gaining the reliability on the promised date of delivery.
- Simplifying the production process control.
- Reducing the number of rejects upon final inspection.
- Building up the confidence of customers and distributors.
- Utilising the plant spaces more effectively, thus facilitating the handling and transporting in the plant.
- Removing drastically unnecessary work from supervisors' assignments.
- Helping employees in gaining confidence and pride in their work.
- Making workers readily take prompt remedial actions.
- Allowing supervisors more spare time to take care of other important work.
- Growth of project team activities through gaining experience.

Yamaha

On a recent IFS study tour to Japan, Alan Harrison, of the University of Warwick School of Industrial and Business Studies, was asked to record his impressions of JIT at Yamaha.

Applying just-in-time principles to the manufacture of the world's finest grand pianos seems improbable. For a start, there are many human judgements which need to be made. The craftsman has to gauge the water content of a wood, the tone is adjusted by delicately pricking the hammers, and only the human ear can fine tune the instrument. Then, you can hardly build only as needed when the product lead time is several years and demand is extremely seasonal.

And yet Yamaha is facing intense competition, particularly from the South Koreans, whose wage rate is just 20% of that in Japan. The response has been to compete on quality, not on price. Yamaha has emphasised its appeal to the concert pianist and solo artist to promote its image. Uprights and baby grands are produced also at its 11 overseas factories to keep costs down, but the company skilfully exploits just-in-time principles, combining high technology with the human touch. Both are needed, and both have to be used in each operation. Where possible, it uses automation.

Quality. The two main factors influencing quality are:

- *Choice of the right raw materials. For example, spruce is the best wood for the soundboard and is imported from Rumania and Alaska.*
- *Stabilisation of the natural products used in piano construction. These are primarily wood, leather and felt. The raw wood is seasoned for up to 2 years in the open air, then in a scientifically controlled seasoning chamber.*

Yamaha has also introduced at its Iwata factory vacuum shield mould casting of the frames, giving exceptional strength and precision.

Production Control. Several factors have to be balanced, including:

- *Variety. Although there are only 10 basic specifications, this increases with colours and wood types to 200 varieties. These include the 'C' and 'G' series, and the top-of-the-range CFIII series which retails at Y≠m.*
- *Seasonality. The Japanese school year starts in April and bonus payments in June and December create demand peaks. December is accentuated by Christmas in export markets.*
- *Wood treatment. Four grades of wood seasoning are used to adjust the product to different world climates.*
- *Lead time of raw materials. Wood is purchased 1 year ahead of*

demand, and seasoning takes over 2 years (75% of the piano body is wood).

Pianos are built to forecast, on a 6-month planning horizon. The company wants to reduce the forecast period to 4 months, but this is proving difficult. As a trade-off it carres 1.5 to 2 months' inventory of finished product.

The main factory at Hamamatsu builds 100 grand pianos per day and has applied flow techniques to both the main assembly and subassemblies. The factory is well-lit, with painted or polished wood floors, and is very orderly. Everyone, including managers, wears blue trousers and pale blue shirts and caps. Several operators wear badges proclaiming 'challenge 90' – a drive for a 30% efficiency improvement each year to 1990.

The process route for assembly is shown in Fig. 2.7. The operations are briefly:

- *Frame preparation. Drilling and tapping operations on the cast-iron frame.*
- *Soundboard and frame to support posts. The curved and straight support posts have been assembled and polished at the Tenryu factory. Here, the soundboard and frame are securely fastened.*

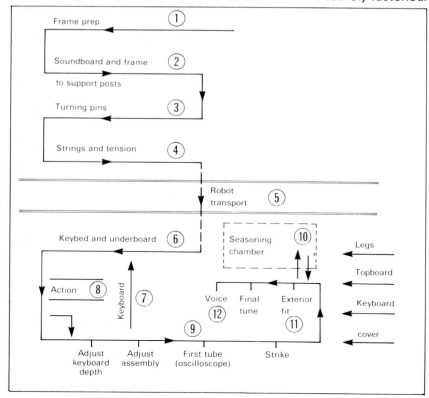

Fig. 2.7 Flow in manufacture of grand pianos

Fig. 2.8 Insertion of tuning pins

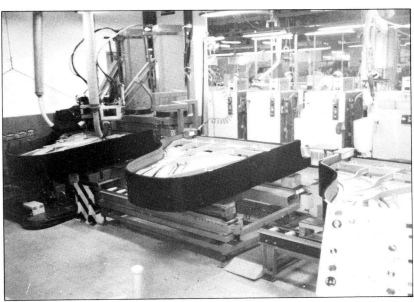

● *Tuning pins. Yamaha robots drill holes in the frame (see Fig. 2.8) and insert the tuning pins to the correct torque.*

● *Strings and tension. Two hundred and thirty strings are fitted to the tuning pins, each tensioned to 90 kg.*

● *Transport. The piano body is conveyed by robot across the road to final assembly, warning pedestrians with an electronic tune.*

● *Keybed and underboard. These are fastened to the body.*

● *Keyboard. This is prepared as a subassembly and placed in the body to take it to the final adjustment.*

● *Action. This is assembled in a series of flowlines. Its design has not changed in over 100 years.*

● *Final adjustment. Height and depth of the keyboard are adjusted by laser measurement. The first tuning is carried out by oscilloscope. An automatic string machine hits each key 600 times to cause warpage.*

● *Seasoning. The piano is seasoned for a week to stabilise the strings and action.*

● *Exterior fit. Legs, pedals and top board are fitted. A floor pit makes it easy for the operator to fit the legs.*

● *Tune and voice. The last operations are human touches to final-tune the piano and to adjust each hammer by delicately pricking and sounding it to perfect the 'voice'.*

Production of grand pianos at Yamaha is an unusual example of the application of 'nagare'. Both manual and automated operations exist in the flowline, with extraordinary balance and rhythm. Everywhere is evidence of attention to detail to make the operator's task as easy as possible.

Checklists

Japanese companies make extensive use of checklists to focus attention on areas of potential improvement. A typical Muda, Muri, Mura checklist would look like this:*

3-MU checklist of Kaizen activities

Muda (waste)	Muri (strain)	Mura (discrepancy)
1. Manpower	1. Manpower	1. Manpower
2. Technique	2. Technique	2. Technique
3. Method	3. Method	3. Method
4. Time	4. Time	4. Time
5. Facilities	5. Facilities	5. Facilities
6. Jigs and tools	6. Jigs and tools	6. Jigs and tools
7. Materials	7. Materials	7. Materials
8. Production volume	8. Production volume	8. Production volume
9. Inventory	9. Inventory	9. Inventory
10. Place	10. Place	10. Place
11. Way of thinking	11. Way of thinking	11. Way of thinking

Two other commonly used checklists are the five Ws/1H and the 4-M:

The five Ws/1H

Who	What	Where
1. Who does it?	1. What to do?	1. Where to do it?
2. Who is doing it?	2. What is being done?	2. Where is it done?
3. Who should be doing it?	3. What should be done?	3. Where should it be done?
4. Who else can do it?	4. What else can be done?	4. Where else can it be done?
5. Who else should do it?	5. What else should be done?	5. Where else should it be done?
6. Who is doing 3-MUs?	6. What 3-MUs are being done?	6. Where are 3-MUs being done?

When	Why	How
1. When to do it?	1. Why does he do it?	1. How to do it?
2. When is it done?	2. Why do it?	2. How is it done?
3. When should it be done?	3. Why do it there?	3. How should it be done?
4. What other time should it be done?	4. Why do it then?	4. Can this method be used in other areas?
5. What other time should it be done?	5. Why do it that way?	5. Is there any other way to do it?
6. Are there any time 3-MUs?	6. Are there any 3-MUs in the way of thinking?	6. Are there any 3-MUs in the method?

*From *Kaizen: the Key to Japan's Competitive Success*, by Masaaki Imai. © 1986 by the Kaizen Institute, Ltd. Reprinted by permission of Random House, Inc.

The 4-M checklist

A. Man (operator)	B. Machine (facilities)
1. Does he follow standards?	1. Does it meet production requirements?
2. Is his work efficiency acceptable?	2. Does it meet process capabilities?
3. Is he problem-conscious?	3. Is the oiling (greasing) adequate?
4. Is he responsible? (Is he accountable?)	4. Is the inspection adequate?
5. Is he qualified?	5. Is operation stopped often because of mechanical trouble?
6. Is he experienced?	6. Does it meet precision requirements?
7. Is he assigned to the right job?	7. Does it make any unusual noises?
8. Is he willing to improve?	8. Is the layout adequate?
9. Does he maintain good human relations?	9. Are there enough machines/facilities?
10. Is he healthy?	10. Is everything in good working order?

C. Material	D. Operation method
1. Are there any mistakes in volume?	1. Are the work standards adequate?
2. Are there any mistakes in grade?	2. Is the work standard upgraded?
3. Are there any mistakes in the brand name?	3. Is it a safe method?
4. Are there impurities mixed in?	4. Is it a method that ensures a good product?
5. Is the inventory level adequate?	5. Is it an efficient method?
6. Is there any waste in material?	6. Is the sequence of work adequate?
7. Is the handling adequate?	7. Is the set-up adequate?
8. Is the work-in-progress abandoned?	8. Are the temperature and humidity adequate?
9. Is the layout adequate?	9. Are the lighting and ventilation adequate?
10. Is the quality standard adequate?	10. Is there adequate contact with the previous and following processes?

3. JIT in the United States

Companies in the United States adopted JIT initially as a defence against Japanese encroachment on their domestic and international markets. However, the US manufacturing culture's stress on planning has proved an obstacle in many cases. In this chapter, we compare US and Japanese approaches to JIT, and examine some of the US successes.

3 JIT in the United States

The evolution of US JIT

According to some observers, JIT owes its origins to Henry Ford I. When he built his model T factory, the mass production principles included a continuous flow of materials from pressed steel to final assembly along what was for the times a highly automated line. The cycle time for production within the factory – when all went well – was a remarkable 72 hours. Explains US JIT consultant Richard Schonberger:

> In 1923/4, the massive River Rouge Island Park facilities of Ford had very high levels of quality, perhaps not quite up to today's standard of parts per million but quite excellent. Also, in the Ford system there was a very high level of preventive maintenance. The machines could not break down because these plants operated without warehouses, without buffer stocks. There was little room for error if the machines broke down. And also, the Ford system at that time was extremely simple – so simple in fact that suppliers to the Ford enterprise were delivering multiple times per day just in time, without invoices, without the complications and the red tape and the paperwork of invoices.

Yet Ford's achievement lacked two vital ingredients of JIT as we define it today. The first is it had very little flexibility. It was designed around a single, standard product with minimal variety of accessories. When the customers' expectations changed and they wanted different colours, different upholstery and other refinements, the system found it increasingly difficult to cope. General Motors, which could provide greater flexibility, took over market leadership.

The second missing ingredient was the human input. Says Schonberger:

> One of Henry Ford's biographies said something like this: 'Man No. 1 puts a bolt in the hole but does not put a nut on it. Man No. 2 puts a nut on the bolt but does not tighten it down. Man No. 3 finally tightens the nut on the bolt.' Now that is about as far away from my concept of employee involvement as I can imagine. Those employees in the Ford concept of mass production were cogs in the machine, little else. This was a weakness: it took many years for companies in the automobile industry to learn how to tap the brain power and the hands-on experience of the people on the factory floor, in the quest for continual improvement.

In many respects, Henry Ford's approach still colours US attitudes towards manufacturing today. Inevitably, this has an impact on the acceptability of JIT techniques and how US companies use them.

While Japanese companies in the 1960s were concentrating on JIT, their US counterparts were focusing their efforts on materials requirements planning (MRP). It was essentially a difference of philosophy: the US companies believed – and in many cases still do believe – that improving the efficiency of planning was the best way of achieving continuous production flow and controlling inventory.

The achievements of MRP and its successor techniques MRP II should not be underestimated. Many Japanese companies have adopted these approaches with equal enthusiasm, even though they were fully aware of what JIT can do. Frequently, JIT and MRP can be seen in the same Japanese factory, where they are regarded as supportive, rather than exclusive, activities.

Extent of current awareness and practice of JIT in the United States

US companies that have adopted JIT, or derivatives of it, often create their own names for the approach. Omark Industries, of Oregon, calls its system ZIPS (zero inventory production system); plastics products maker T.D. Shea Manufacturing, of Michigan, has a nick-of-time programme; motorcycle manufacturer Harley-Davidson Motor Co. has MAN (material-as-needed). Few companies – in manufacturing at least – can be aware of JIT and its potential benefits.

JIT consultants in the United States advise Fortune 500 companies such as Westinghouse, Motorola and Black & Decker, as well as small 20-employee manufacturers. However, most implementation is by large companies, who have the purchasing muscle to oblige their suppliers to change their behaviour.

One of the most recent comparative studies of JIT attitudes and practices in the United States and Japan – so recent in fact that, at time of writing, only preliminary conclusions were available – has been conducted by Robert Hall of Indiana University and Jinichiro Nakane of Japan's Waseda University. The study* compared companies in both countries in three industry sectors: automotive, diesel engine and minicomputer. Its primary observations were:

● In each case, Japanese manufacturing strategy was clearer than American. Japanese stressed flexibility; Americans stressed cost and quality.
● Americans and Japanese understand JIT differently: Japanese as a direction whereby the people of the company are strengthened; Americans as more as a set of techniques.

---

*'Developing flexibility for excellence in manufacturing – preliminary results of a Japanese-American study', by R.W Hall and J. Nakane, an unpublished paper delivered on 11 March 1988, Dearborn, Michigan. The study was inspired by the Association for Manufacturing Excellence and funded by Arthur Young & Co.

- To improve flexibility by reducing lead times of all activities, companies in both countries need a strong corporate culture and a fluid organisation structure.
- Japanese had been more successful in promoting flexibility with suppliers.

Supplier issues prove far more intractable for US manufacturers than their Japanese counterparts. While daily delivery was the norm for 'JIT' Japanese the companies, the US manufacturers had at most a handful of daily suppliers. One reason for this is that counterpart US companies' suppliers tended to be located at greater distances (on average, 5–10 times further away). More significant, however, is the lack of a network of suppliers who can respond rapidly to changes. Personal interaction between Japanese companies and their suppliers was more developed than in the US. From this, two other practices of the Japanese assisted supplier flexibility. The first was to source families of parts from the same suppliers. The second was to develop 'family' resources to deal promptly and efficiently with tooling and equipment problems. In general, the contractual relationships of the US companies, which place liability (and therefore responsibility) for tooling problems squarely with the supplier, discouraged this kind of involvement and sharing of know-how.

The report also comments on the degree of involvement of top management: 'The top American executives have not felt the need to continuously repeat goals. They speak more through a hierarchy''. Japanese executives exhort everyone in the company.

Other observers of recent US manufacturing history, such as consultant Dr Leonard Bertain or Harvard's Professor Robert Hayes, trace the evolution of the US approach to a style of business established in the 1940s, where short-term gains became increasingly important in top management strategy. Inevitably, this philosophy inhibited radical manufacturing change, because long-term investments were more difficult to justify. To a considerable extent, this situation persists in many companies. However, Bertain argues strongly that large numbers of companies have been stimulated by the Japanese challenge to go back to basics and rethink their manufacturing approach and strategy.

In adopting JIT, US firms have applied their own concepts, to adapt it to the realities of doing business in a very different culture. Among the changes:

- Some companies now refer to JIT as 'added-value manufacture', a term which is more acceptable to US senior management and, arguably, more accurately descriptive of the objectives of the approach.
- Although they have in many cases drastically reduced the numbers of suppliers, in large part through quality accreditation schemes,

the concept of single-sourcing is a definite taboo. The reasons given are usually to promote competition and innovation among suppliers.

● Some US companies have negotiated no-strike deals with their suppliers' workforces. For the unions, 'no-stock manufacturing' has become a useful bargaining point. For the purchasing manufacturer, guaranteed supplies carry a significant value.

Successful applications of JIT in the United States

As happened subsequently with total quality management, the first US companies to adopt JIT techniques tended to be either Japanese companies with US subsidiaries or US companies with successful Japanese subsidiaries. One of the first examples, described in some detail by Richard Schonberger, the US JIT guru,* was Kawasaki Heavy Industries, which adopted JIT at its US plant in Lincoln, Nebraska in 1980. The plant, which makes motorcycles and other leisure vehicles, had begun preparations to introduce a long-term and expensive materials requirements planning system. It abandoned those plans in favour of JIT, on the grounds that it would achieve the same results at lower cost and in less implementation time, if experience in the company's Japanese plants was anything to go by.

The initial attempts to introduce a Kanban style of production to the motorcycle final assembly line failed miserably, because they were introduced in isolation. The experience convinced the plant's managers that JIT had to be seen in a much wider context – that productivity improvement came through applying a whole range of JIT tools and techniques within an integrated programme. Among the measures taken, records Schonberger:*

All of the Kawasaki managers were challenged to develop ways to cut inventories and move toward just-in-time operations. The purchasing manager trained all of his buyers in JIT purchasing, and the buyers in turn worked on ways to effect small, more frequent deliveries of bought materials. Within the plant, punch presses were outfitted with platforms made of roller conveyors so that heavy dies could be changed in minutes rather than hours. A welding shop was converted from a general-purpose welding booth configuration to several welding production lines, each dedicated to welding frames for a certain size of motorcycle, with frames moving piece by piece down the welding lines. A differential subassembly shop was physically moved to a position where it could feed differentials 'just-in-time' to the using station

*Japanese Manufacturing Techniques, by R. Schonberger, The Free Press, New York, 1982.
*Op. cit.

on the assembly line for three-wheel motorcycles. The receiving procedure for parts coming from Japan was changed to a dock-to-line flow pattern, which eliminated 60 percent of the storage racks, and the space was turned over to manufacturing.

At the same time, the plant manager encapsulated the overall goal in terms that everyone could respond to. The entire plant was 'a series of stations on the assembly line, whether physically there or not'. Subsequent actions initiated by a new Japanese management brought in other familiar aspects of Japanese JIT assembly, including the installation of trouble lights at each assembly station and the progressive dismantling of conveyor belts.

Within 2 years, and in spite of a major recession in its industry sector, the Kawasaki plant had raised productivity and reduced costs significantly. It had also moved from batch production to full mixed model manufacturing – every motorcycle is made to order as a batch of one. It did so ahead of the company's main Japanese production facility in Akashi.

Significantly, Schonberger and other US consultants see JIT and quality control as inextricably linked. They bracket the two concepts together – along with others – under the term 'world class manufacturing'.

More recent examples of successful use of JIT include valve manufacturer Amot Controls, electronics manufacturer Opcon and McDonnell Douglas Computer Systems Co. Amot Controls, based in Richmond, Virginia, is a small company making thermostatic valves for diesel engines. It employs 180 people and turns over $20 million a year. Its 12 major products are seasonal and have as many as 75 000 possible permutations. There are some 16 000 active components in its inventory. Given this kind of background, it is not surprising that its primary objective in embarking upon JIT in 1986 was to gain greater control over its manufacturing processes, rather than simply to reduce inventory.

Amot redesigned its assembly areas and the machine shops into cells, with the aid of the operatives themselves. The cells each concentrate on a family of products and its variations. Families are grouped not by physical shape or size, but by the processes required for their manufacture. At the operator's hand are all the tools, drawings and gauges needed for that family of products. The output of the cells is controlled by manning levels and by a Kanban system. It still uses a form of materials requirements planning for generating rough schedules, but not for controlling the work within the cells. Speed of throughput has been raised by reducing setting times and, in some cases, by investment in duplicate equipment.

Amot preaches a simple message to its workforce:

● Understand the process/problem.

- Simplify it.
- Computerise/automate only when necessary.

This philosophy has saved it major expenditures in automatic plant and flexible manufacturing systems, which just proved unnecessary. The results speak for themselves. The company has:

- *Reduced* direct manufacturing time by 57%.
- *Reduced* WIP in manufacturing cells from 5 days to 3 minutes.
- *Increased* sales turnover by 20%, using 20% less labour and 30% less floor space.

Opcon is also a small company, employing 100 people in the manufacture of photoelectric sensors and control equipment for factory automation, particularly in the food industry. It has not had an easy ride implementing JIT, but in overcoming its problems, it has generated a number of innovatory solutions to making the financial systems support the JIT effort.

Two years ago, Opcon was in serious trouble. It was losing business because it could not meet customers' requirements for quality, lead times and product variation. It was turning over capital employed less than twice a year. Two years of attempts to introduce JIT with the aid of Japanese advisers had failed because the Japanese culture did not fit.

A new vice president of manufacturing, with extensive experience of JIT in a US environment, took charge and determined to force JIT implementation through. A large part of the solution to making JIT stick lay in the accounting practices. The accounts department's resistance to throughput accounting (throughput accounting bases cost and inventory calculations on the amount that passes through production, rather than on material booked in and out of stock) in favour of traditional accounting methods that stress return on investment, was overcome by running both systems in parallel. The data from throughput accounting provide the feedback that tells operators and managers how well they are doing. Information on the previous day's sales output, margins, debtors, creditors, inventory levels and cash flow is now posted on the factory noticeboard daily by 09.00, alongside information on quality levels and productivity. The employees are interested in these data because their bonuses depend upon them. Employees who achieve 100% quality for a 3–5 month period qualify for a rolling $100 bonus. At the same time, their productivity bonus is tied to achieving 98% quality.

This transparency of information has had additional benefits in terms of manning levels. The direct employees themselves adjust the manning levels of the production cells, depending upon their assessment of the daily requirements. If extra labour is required, they requisition it. However, because their salaries are directly related to productivity, they have every incentive to keep manning levels under close control.

Successful implementation of JIT has plainly reversed Opcon's downhill slide. Instead of laying workers off, it is now reassigning workers to cope with the extra sales. Much of this sales increase relates to higher quality product; but much also comes from having the capability to assemble product to the customer's specification. (Batch manufacture having now been eliminated, all products are custom-made.) Other significant improvements include:

- Major increases in productivity (one department registered an improvement of 58.7% in 7 months).
- A reduction in average lead time through the manufacturing process from 8 weeks to 1 day. Lead time from a customer's order to despatch is now 4 days.

McDonnell Douglas's computer systems division, which makes minicomputers, is a medium-sized company employing 1500 people worldwide. Of these, only 350 work in the manufacturing operation at Irving, California. It had very clear goals in embracing JIT. Top management wanted to *reduce*:

- Set-up times.
- Lot sizes.
- Materials handling.
- Paperwork.
- Move distances.
- Number of suppliers.
- Number of parts.
- Job classifications.

It wanted to *increase*:

- Process quality.
- Product quality.
- Process flexibility.
- People flexibility.
- Communication.
- Productivity.
- Teamwork.
- Innovation.

It sent an executive team out to visit JIT facilities in other companies around the world. Based on their recommendations and the advice of a consultant, the company installed a pilot JIT unit and invested heavily in training for everyone who would be involved, from top management down. The results were dramatic. Within the first 11 months, from July 1986, the following improvements occurred:

- Manufacturing inventories (without write-offs)   −19%
- Manufacturing inventories (with write-offs)   −25%
- Rework   −37%
- Work-in-progress (WIP) investment   −34%
- Throughput time circuit board assembly (3–6 days)   −50%
- Subassembly stockroom (emptied)   −2100sq.ft
- Component move distance (1 mile–100ft)   5180ft
- Yield (electro-mechanical) 95–99%   +80%
- Yield (manual insertion) 68–92%   +75%
- Man hours/ststem– productivity   +40%
- Money accrued from consumption of excess WIP   = $574 000
- Housekeeping – clear aisles, uncluttered work stations, etc.

In many cases, JIT is seen either as a next step from total quality management or as a parallel development. Hewlett-Packard and Xerox have both taken this approach, with remarkable results. Of Hewlett Packard's 52 divisions, approximately half have adopted JIT. The results within just four of those divisions are reproduced in Table 1.

Table 1

H-P Greeley Division		H-P Fort Collins Division	
Inventory reduction	2.8 months to 1.3 months	Inventory reduction	75%
Labour cost reduction	30%	Labour cost reduction	15%
Space reduction	50%	Space reduction	30%
WIP stock reduction	22 days to 1 day	Quality improvement	30% scrap/79% rework
Production increase	100%	Throughput time reduction	50%
H-P Computer Systems Division		**H-P. Vancouver Division**	
Standard hours reduction	50%	WIP inventory reduction	82%
Material scrap reduction	80%	Space reduction	40%
Space reduction	33%	Scrap/rework reduction	30%
Through-out time reduction	17 days to 30 hours	Labour efficiency increase	50%
Inventory reduction	75%	No. of shipments increase	20%

But H-P is far from satisfied. It sees its achievements so far as merely first steps on a very long road. A major part of its efforts, particularly at its pioneering Vancouver plant, has gone into educating employees, on the grounds that the priorities in implementing JIT have to be people, then processes, then systems.

In general, those US companies which have implemented JIT with enthusiasm and commitment, seem to have more than recovered their investment. John Proud, of Xerox Computer Services, compiled the following list of paybacks achieved by the most successful JIT companies in the United States:

- Manufacturing lead times reduced — 80–90%
- Productivity increases (direct) — 5–50%
- Productivity increases (indirect) — 20–60%
- Purchase price reduction — 5–10%
- Inventory reductions
  - Raw materials — 35–75%
  - WIP — 30–90%
  - Finished goods — 50–90%
- Set-up reduction — 75–95%
- Space reduction — 40–80%
- Quality improvements — 50–55%
- Material stockouts reduction — 50–95%
- Scrap reductions — 20–30%

The downside: problems and failures

While success in these and many other companies has been well-publicised – some of them having cut production lead times (the time to transform raw materials into finished goods) 10- or even 20-fold – they nonetheless represent only a vanguard of manufacturing. A US study in 1985 found that 41% of manufacturing companies in the major city surveyed admitted to being completely ignorant of JIT.

The majority of US manufacturing companies are still investing in traditional methods of factory organisation. In particular, huge sums are still being spent on automated materials storage and handling. Says Schonberger:*

This automates the excesses between the processes where value is added, and it deprives the plant of that much capital for improving the processes themselves. Distance-spanning conveyors, accumulators, and automated storage systems belong in distribution centres, but in factories they are physical impediments to making an improvement and to linking processes more closely together to create teams. Furthermore, they consume support staff and overhead costs.

The world-class manufacturers are tearing out their racks, conveyors, and storage systems as fast as their confused and endangered competitors are putting them in. For example, Zytec, rapidly improving small manufacturer headquartered in Minneapolis, has two warehouses, but one holds nothing but containers, racks, conveyors, pallets, and the like – torn out of their plant and ready for sale or disposal, at which time Zytec will terminate its lease on the warehouse.

*'World-class manufacturing trends', in *JIT – an Executive Briefing*, edited by J. Mortimer, IFS Publications, Bedford, 1987.

Moreover, a significant but unquantified proportion of US companies that *have* begun to use JIT have found that their programmes have run out of steam. The reasons are numerous and include the following, according to Schonberger:

● *Failure to gain commitment.* 'In most US organisations the casualty rate of abandoned ideas is high. Time is not taken to gain consensus. Therefore:

 ○ Many doubters remain, and they passively or actively resist.
 ○ Issues outside the area of expertise of the innovator are not properly considered, which makes decisions somewhat prone to failure, whether there is resistance or not.'†

● *Loss of a 'champion'.* 'One or two forceful JIT champions are transferred, and JIT stalls. This should not happen, and it won't if the JIT training effort is broadly conceived. All employees, line and staff, managerial and operator-level, should receive training. Preliminary training can be as brief as watching a 30-minute videotape. Many kinds of secondary training follow, gradually making JIT believers out of most employees.'*

● *Lack of employee involvement.* 'Managers and staff experts are used to being in control and making the decisions. They find it hard to 'release the reins'. Given the limited numbers of managers and experts that a company can afford to employ, rapid improvement cannot be sustained without the full involvement of line employees. Ironically, the most talented and dedicated managers and engineers often are the biggest obstacles to employee involvement – even though intellectually they are likely to see the need for it.'*

● *Lack of 'signboard' controls.* 'Related to this is a lack of devices on the factory floor to make it natural and easy for line employees to be meaningfully involved in the improvement effort. I refer to a variety of signboards on which all process variabilities are recorded – by the operators. The signboards can track hourly performance against an hourly scheduled rate, record causes when a red- or yellow-light condition occurs, display process variation on pre-control or X-bar and R charts, and so forth.'*

● *'Impure' forms of JIT.* 'It has been said many times that the simplification that goes with JIT is excellent preparation for technology – process technology and information system technology. Perhaps it has not been said often enough that the opposite is not true: implementation of process or information system technology is *not* a good way to introduce JIT. Yet some

---

†*Japanese Manufacturing Techniques*, by R. Schonberger, The Free Press, New York, 1982.

*JIT for 'world-class' manufacturing, by R. Schonberger, *Proceedings 3rd International Conference on Just-in-Time Manufacturing*, IFS Publications, Bedford, 1988.

consultants, vendors, and even some articles and books have advocated costly automated equipment or an information system that supposedly will at the same time achieve the goals of JIT. Some companies have followed that advice. The result is an impure form of JIT that did not involve line operators in its implementation and probably does not involve them much in its use. Another result is creation of a large overhead empire to install and run the technology.'*

To this list can be added the problems created by the traditional Western organisation structure. Unless companies are prepared to break down departmental barriers and create more flexible organisations, they will find it difficult to reap the full benefits of JIT or to obtain commitment across the company. As Hall and Nakane express it in their comparative study: several American 'JIT companies' now recognise that traditional organisation structures are among the biggest inhibitors of progress. They promote procedure, delay and much waiting for specialists, rather than promoting great shrinkage of lead times. The problem has been described as 'the functional silo syndrome'.

Case examples

The NUMMI production system†

NUMMI (New United Motor Manufacturing Inc.) is a joint venture company established by General Motors Corporation and Toyota Motor Corporation to manufacture subcompact automobiles in the United States. Their Fremont, California plant is located at a site abandoned by General Motors. It is highly automated, with 90 % of welds being made by robots. It has a final assembly line 1.3 miles long, making 60 vehicles an hour.

The joint owners decided that there was much to be gained by blending the best of US and Japanese manufacturing culture. To achieve this, they arranged an 'educational exchange'. Three hundred group and team leaders from NUMMI went to Japan for 3 weeks' training; 200 Toyota workers from Japan came to California to train NUMMI employees. Toyota also sent 24 'co-ordinators' to asist managers and team leaders in implementing the Toyota production system.

Key concepts in the process include:

● *Heijunka.* This is smoothing of variety and volume in the production process by levelling their fluctuations over time; from minutes, to hours, to days, to weeks, to months, to years. Through the

---

*JIT for 'world-class' manufacturing, by R. Schonberger, *Proceedings 3rd International Conference on Just-in-Time Manufacturing*, IFS Publications, Bedford, 1988.

†This case study includes extracts from "Car manufacturing joint venture test feasibility of Toyota methods in US", **Industrial Engineering**, March 1986.

application of a computerised algorithm, the vehicle orders are lined up to reflect the ratio of model and option penetration in the total incoming orders. Therefore, if automatic transmission penetration is 65% and manual transmission is 35%, air conditioning 70%, power steering 80%, etc. the vehicle build sequence will closely reflect these ratios individually and in combination.

● *Total quality*. Whether on the production line or in the office, each team member is required to pass on to the following operation only 100% quality output. Where possible, through the principle of Jidoka, mechanical processes have automated quality checking to identify out of specification conditions. Every team member, as his or her own quality inspector, is encouraged to 'stop the line to not stop the line': This means that if a problem is encountered the line can be stopped, the problem addressed and counter measures taken, and it should not be necessary to stop the line again for the same problem.

● *Standardised work*. Each team member's tasks are studied and a standardised work chart is developed, which visually depicts the actions required to complete the tasks – including work operations, quality checks, walking, waiting, movement of materials, etc. By measuring the time required for each action, the net time for a team member's total standardised work can be known. This net time can be compared to task time (daily total operating time at 100% efficiency/required total production) to assist in workforce planning and efficiency improvements.

● *Kanban*. At New United Motor, there are many types of Kanban. In-process and signal Kanban are mainly used in the stamping plant and in the body/welding operations. Inter-process and supplier Kanban are used throughout the manufacturing operations. The Kanban forms and formats vary according to need. An electronic computer-to-computer signal functions as a Kanban between NUMMI and its Japan supplier. Triangular metal Kanbans are used in the stamping plant. Both reusable and disposable paper Kanbans are used in component ordering and delivery. Where applicable, the data on the Kanban are bar-coded to facilitate data collection. If the data change frequently, the information is handwritten and can be easily revised.

● *Small lot sizes*. One major problem faced by the plant is the need to import many components from Japan. NUMMI provides Toyota Japan with forecasts of bulk orders 4 months ahead. These orders are incorporated into Toyota's domestic production forecasts.

For packaging and transportation, Toyota has devised a system that classifies container loads in two ways. 'B' containers contain parts specified by option, Katashiki (basic vehicle model) and option, or option combination, and standard fasteners. 'A' containers contain

Katashiki specified parts, with parts for only one kind of Katashiki in a particular container.

Local supply systems operate much as in Toyota's domestic plants. New United Motor has 75 suppliers in North America supplying some 700 parts for the Nova. While 55 of these suppliers are located in the mid-West, there are six suppliers in the southeast, three in Mexico and 11 in California. These suppliers are considered part of the NUMMI team, and operate in an atmosphere of mutual trust and respect, with the concepts of the NUMMI production system used to govern the supplier relationship. As this type of automotive manufacturer-supplier relationship, while typical in Japan, is not as common in North America, special care was taken in supplier evaluation and selection. Quality, price, location and other normal selection criteria were important, but the attitude of the supplier was the critical factor. Suppliers had to be willing to accept the constraints of a production system that may have been unknown to them, or in most cases was not used between them and their other automotive customers.

To assist the suppliers, NUMMI sends team members from Production Control, Quality, Manufacturing and Purchasing in groups to visit suppliers. These team members provide training, assist in problem solving, practice Kaizen, and in general, work to strengthen the NUMMI–supplier relationship. Periodic supplier conferences are held to discuss common issues and provide information concerning future events.

The packaging for components supplied by North American suppliers was designed by Toyota to provide optimum protection during shipment, maximise space and weight utilisation during transportation, contain the quantity of parts compatible with hourly delivery to lineside and fit the in-plant material handling equipment.

Chrysler Corporation

Chrysler's new plant at Sterling Heights, Michigan, produces 60 cars an hour in two shifts, and some 70% of the vehicles' parts-value arrive just in time.[*] The plant's JIT programme has four major elements, as follows:

● *Improved containerisation.* All packaging was redesigned to maximise efficiency. In place of hazardous and wasteful wood and cardboard containers, the plant now uses steel and plastic. Many of the racks and bins are collapsible, to reduce storage needs. A bonus is that one returning truck can transport several loads of empties. Chrysler estimates it has eliminated annually 6500 tonnes of waste packaging materials.

*"Four ways Chrysler backs JIT with handling efficiency", *Modern Materials Handling* July 1985.

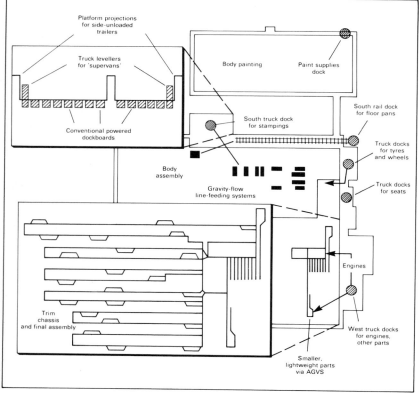

Labels within figure:
- Platform projections for side-unloaded trailers
- Truck levellers for 'supervans'
- Conventional powered dockboards
- Body painting
- Paint supplies dock
- South rail dock for floor pans
- South truck dock for stampings
- Truck docks for tyres and wheels
- Body assembly
- Truck docks for seats
- Gravity-flow line-feeding systems
- Engines
- Trim chassis and final assembly
- West truck docks for engines, other parts
- Smaller, lightweight parts via AGVS

Fig. 3.1 Chrysler's point-of-use concept in which dock areas have been situated close to areas where components will be used. (Source: Modern Materials Handling, July 1985, reproduced by kind permission of Cahners Publishing division of Reed Publishing USA)

- *Faster unloading*. Instead of a single loading area, the plant has multiple docks, situated to be close to the area of the line, where the components will be used (Fig. 3.1).
- *Faster transportation to the line*. The short distance from the docking area to the line means that many parts can be delivered where they are needed by forklift truck. Most small parts are delivered by automatically guided vehicles (AGVs). Current plans involve linking the docking areas for seat deliveries directly to the line via an automated unloading and feeding system that pulls components in as needed. Under normal operation, a vehicle will be emptied and reloaded with empty containers within 10 minutes.
- *Parts accessibility on the line*. Most stations are supplied by gravity feed. As a container is emptied, it is released and falls into a lower level, where it is collected and recycled.

All of this activity – some 270 trailerloads and eight railcars a day – is monitored via 1000 production data terminals at work stations. The materials handling savings alone are expected to amount to $10 million a year.

4. JIT in the United Kingdom

The UK's response to JIT has been very similar to that of the United States. There are many barriers to implementation arising from cultural factors and misconceptions about the nature of JIT. However, there are also numerous success stories.

4 JIT in the United Kingdom

UK manufacturing and JIT: an overview

UK companies have, by and large, accepted the need for change in manufacturing processes. They are, at the same time, highly cautious of rapid or radical change. This caution has meant that, while awareness of JIT is relatively high, commitment to implementation is far less forthcoming.

This view is borne out strongly by two major surveys. The first, by Warwick University's School of Industrial and Business Studies, found that 57% of a sample of 123 companies are implementing or have implemented some aspects of JIT, and 59% felt they had a good understanding of the approach. Nonetheless, only 16% had a formal programme to investigate or implement it.

Table 4.1 shows how those companies that have either considered JIT, or begun to implement it, have focused their efforts. A number of items stand out from this table. First, the high proportion of companies who are looking for and have implemented flexibility in the workforce. Second, the small number of companies which have implemented what might be termed the core techniques of JIT, such as cellular manufacturing, statistical process control, U-shaped lines, schedule smoothing and Kanban. Kanban, the best known of all the techniques, comes bottom in actual implementation and next to bottom in planned implementation. It would seem, from the data in this table, that fewer than 15% of companies in the sample have implemented a wide set of JIT approaches or techniques. Even the majority of the companies planning or implementing JIT have considered only a partial approach.

Table 4.1 Company activities in JIT

Technique	Implemented by % of total sample	Planned, implementing or implemented
1. Flexible workforce	30.1	80.0
2. WIP reduction	18.7	67.1
3. Product simplification	16.2	60.0
4. Preventive maintenance	11.4	60.0
5. Statistical process control	13.8	58.6
6. Set-up time reduction	16.2	54.3
7. Continuous improvement	11.4	54.3
8. JIT purchasing	15.4	51.4
9. Work team quality control	11.4	50.0
10. Standard containers	15.4	44.3
11. Modules or cells	11.4	44.3
12. Zero defects	3.2	34.3
13. Mixed modelling	8.9	31.4
14. Smoothed line build rate	9.7	25.7
15. Parallel lines	10.6	22.9
16. U-shaped lines	9.7	22.9
17. Kanban	4.1	11.4
	n=123	n=70 (56.9%)

It may also be significant that the measures which rank at the upper levels are generally easier to implement than some of the measures at the lower levels, which entail a stronger commitment to the JIT concept. Clearly the introduction of measures such as Kanban or U-shaped lines requires substantial rearrangement of the production facilities. The comments made by companies interviewed support this assumption. Many companies are implementing individual aspects of JIT rather than the whole concept. However, this should not be construed as a negative statement; clearly there is considerable interest in the subject and the very essence of JIT is to strive continuously for improvement.

UK companies who had implemented JIT were given a list of possible benefits and were asked to rank them. The results are shown in Table 4.2. Another significant survey was by management consultants Price Waterhouse, who surveyed 60 large manufacturing companies in the north west of England. It found that three-quarters had either already begun to introduce elements of JIT or were planning to do so. About 60% were installing or planning to install total quality management. It found, however, that these companies' ability to obtain the maximum benefit from their JIT investments was often constrained by obsolete accounting practices. Price Waterhouse explains:

> In theory, the objectives of JIT all work towards a common goal. Every product should be designed to meet criteria of lowest cost and highest standards of quality and produced only according to demand. The rest of the philosophy follows on from there. Clearly the adoption of such a system represents a fundamental change to the operating strategy of a manufacturing organisation. And this in turn has implications for traditional accounting systems. Specifically, performance measures derived from traditional costing systems represent a barrier to change, because they inhibit the transition to the ideal low-inventory environment.

In support of this argument, the report quotes one surveyed firm which said: 'We know our overall manufacturing costs but we do not know where they are being incurred. It makes planning to cut costs or to increase profitability very difficult.'

Table 4.2   Benefits of JIT

Ranking	Benefit
1	WIP reduction
2	Increased flexibility
3	Raw materials/parts reduction
4	Increased quality
5	Increased productivity
6	Reduced space requirements
7	Lower overheads

Nonetheless, many UK companies are coming to grips with these issues, using JIT as a motivation to improve the cost-effectiveness of their information and control systems across the board. The impact has been substantial in many cases. One company has reduced overall expenditure on management control systems from 4% of turnover to 1.1%, by applying basic principles of JIT to its internal accounting.

The experience of UK manufacturers

Many UK manufacturers now recognise they have a great deal of ground to make up, if they are to compete with their Japanese counterparts. Typical of many small companies is Albion Pressed Metal, of Cannock, Staffs. Says director and general manager, Brian Francis:

The Japanese [in our industry] have invested heavily in sophisticated plant and equipment to reduce labour content. As a presswork company we would have to invest millions to catch up. However, we do have surplus capacity and relatively low labour rates so initially we are converting to very basic cell type manufacture. So far we have reduced setting time for press changeovers from 3 hours to 30 minutes (Fig. 4.1). Our Japanese counterparts are doing it in 3 minutes and aiming for 1 minute. This has got to be our target.

Initial results at Albion have been encouraging. The pilot JIT cells (Fig 4.2a, b) have all recorded improvements in stock levels, quality and scrap and rework. A team bonus scheme adapted from a Japanese model has helped to build a team spirit among the operators, who are now involved in their own maintenance, setting, labouring and quality auditing. The main problems Albion has encountered lie not in the machinery, but with the people issues. Explains Francis: 'Generally, operators are not tuned in to reducing wastes. Also, multiskilling required training and education at all levels.'

Similar experiences can be found in many other JIT-conscious companies in the UK. Declares L.J. Boorman, production engineer at Klippon Electricals in Sheerness, Kent:

The essential problem encountered was one of education. We found that it was most necessary to hold our own in house 'awareness seminars'. In today's world one is continually bombarded with computer programs that are the answer to all problems and to introduce a technique that did not rely on a computer seemed strange. The introduction of JIT relies on cooperation from all levels and it is therefore essential to create

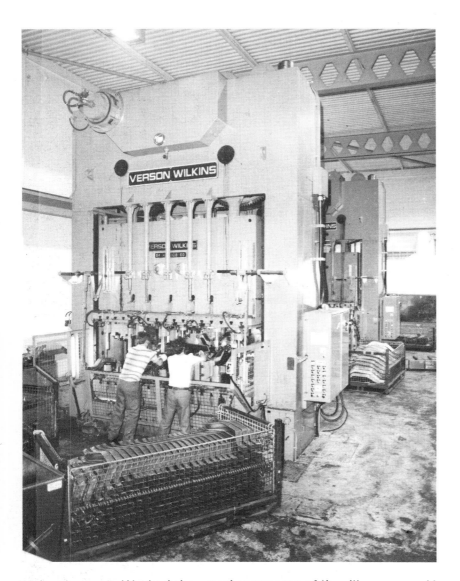

Fig. 4.1 At Albion Pressed Metal setting time for press changeovers has been reduced from 3 hours to 30 minutes

involvement. We had the usual comments of 'it will never work' and 'its all right for the Japanese' along with a great deal more and until we created involvement we made little headway.

Klippon's JIT programme started with the introduction of Kanbans within the production and stores areas (Fig. 4.3) and with investigation of causes of lost production time, particularly in setting up. It had to develop its own system of Kanban, which contains all the information the operator requires for identification, raw material requirements, bin quantity and bagging (Fig. 4.4a, b). But it was able to adopt Japanese lessons in tool change and operation with minimal

Fig. 4.2 Albion Pressed Metal have had encouraging results from the introduction of JIT (a) Spotwelding department before JIT (b) Spotwelding department after JIT

modification. They were, explains Boorman, a matter of 'the philosophy of identification of the problem and using a logical but determined approach'.

It took some time to feel confident enough to remove buffer stocks. Says Boorman:

We have found it necessary to resist pressure to reduce, particularly work in progress and finished stock, until we felt that the time was right and that the mechanism was in place to ensure that deliveries of finished goods were not affected.

We have traditionally always sold from stock and to maintain a high level of service our stocks have always been healthy. Persons become used to seeing full racks of stock and seeing a reduced stock but having confidence that more will arrive as it is required does take time to become the norm. Although we manufacture a large degree of our products in total we do purchase parts and the link to the suppliers for these parts and raw materials is not simple or quick to achieve.

JIT is primarily thought of as a technique for engineering-based companies, with stable production schedules and a reasonably consistent production mix. Yet it is also proving particularly attractive to companies with significant fluctuations in demand. Traditionally, the only way to cope with seasonal peaks of demand has been to maintain substantial stocks and this was the solution lawnmower manufacturer Atco had long used. Around 60% of its sales were in March and April, virtually none in October and November. Although it had survived competition in the 1970s from light mains electric mowers and continued to grow, the Suffolk-based company recognised that it could not compete effectively in the long term unless it reduced its finished stock costs. It also had a number of other problems, associated with the way its product range had been built

Fig. 4.4 (a) An area not subject to JIT, the racks are almost full.
(b) An area after the adoption of JIT, the racks are much less populated.

up. As management consultants A.T. Kearney described it at a recent IFS conference in Germany:*

Expansion has been partially organic and partially by acquisition. The site, located in a mainly agricultural part of Suffolk, has been producing lawnmowers for over 50 years. These two factors lead to

*"JIT in the highly seasonal environment" by S. Young, AT Kearney (UK), Proceedings 4th International Conference on Just-in-Time Manufacturing, IFS Publications Bedford 1988.

a number of complications in manufacturing terms. Commonality of design concepts and of piece parts across product groups is very limited, even down to the level of fastenings. There is an inherited base of aged production machinery and tooling, although there has been significant investment in recent years in c.n.c. machines. The local labour is predominantly from an agricultural, rather than manufacturing background, and the working practices and agreements are fairly traditional. This includes a long established piecework payment by results scheme.

In 1987, Atco management set a manufacturing improvement programme as a central part of its 5-year strategic plan. This is to include every aspect that affects manufacturing such as product and parts rationalisation, quality programmes, CAD/CAM and systems improvements. It chose JIT as the vehicle of change. The highlights of Atco's JIT programme include

- Assembling the majority of products as late as possible, either against order or against accurate short-term forecasts. The critical factor here was to ensure that the product was available when the customer wanted it, because most lawnmowers are purchased in panic rather than by planning. The solution involved improved forecasting, using computer models, while dividing products into those that could be assembled all year round for even plant load and those that could be assembled only on demand.
- Group technology to reduce transport and handling times, supported by investment in automated equipment where appropriate.
- Kanban, with much smaller batch sizes to improve flexibility to sales demand. Batch sizes were reduced in some cases from 3–6 months' cover to 1–8 weeks' cover.
- Rationalisation of suppliers. For example, 30 suppliers of sheet and bar steel have been reduced to three.
- Labour flexibility. The piecework payment by results scheme has been replaced by an added value incentive scheme, which includes indirect workers. In addition, working hours now reflect seasonal effects on plant load.
- A quality programme to improve product design and solve production problems by involving operators.

Similar successes have been recorded in sectors such as food processing, where large peaks and troughs of demand can occur within the same week. In food processing, for example, customer demand for better services is forcing companies to look closely at several areas of performance. Peter Thornton of consultants York MDM lists the critical areas as follows:*

---

*"JIT in the food processing industry" by P. Thornton, York MDM, Proceedings 3rd International Conference on 'Just-in-Time' Manufacturing, IFS Publications 1988.

i) Improved order performance
Customers are increasingly demanding that suppliers meet order requirements not merely in general volume terms, where, accepting an element of product substitution, companies usually score around 98–99% level, but at the individual line item level. When stringent performance measures are applied which take into account the dimensions of individual line item performance (cross-offs), damage free delivery, and accurate supporting paperwork, the performance achieved can fall to as low as 30%.

ii) Improved responsiveness
The trend in the UK towards supermarkets and major retail outlets with limited on-site storage facilities is resulting in requirements for manufacturers, and particularly those of limited shelf life products, to increase the number of drops per week. Given the uneven nature of consumption/sales across the week this implies a concentration of deliveries towards the weekend. Major retailers are consequently talking in terms of three deliveries a week, one early in the week and the second two concentrated towards the run up to the weekend sales peak.

iii) Enhanced product quality
For limited shelf life food products major retailers are gradually beginning to view more frequent deliveries not merely as a method of reducing wasteful inventories but also as a means of improving product 'freshness'. This, of course, implies that suppliers are manufacturing to order rather than supplying from stock. In recognition of the opportunity that exists a number of the most progressive UK retailers are beginning to discuss a requirement not only for more frequent deliveries but also for the product to be manufactured at least twice a week or even to order.

iv) Greater pack option variety
A combination of customers demanding their own pack option and own brand labelling, together with supplier promotional activities, has resulted in a proliferation of pack options. While some segments of the food industry have intermittently fought against this trend and have attemped to control stock keeping unit (SKU) proliferation few have succeeded.

The difficulty is that production cycles in food processing do not normally lend themselves to this kind of operation. Economies of scale have led to mixing and storage systems geared to handling food in bulk, so batches have to be large. Because the equipment is designed for long runs, set-up times tend to be fairly long – speed is the dominant production requirement, not flexibility. Consistency of taste and the need for hygiene also require equipment to be washed down thoroughly between each product or flavour – adding to changeover times. When changeovers do occur they are often accompanied by significant loss of materials while the equipment is brought within tolerance.

One company quoted by Thornton achieved remarkable results by taking a bold JIT approach when it had the opportunity to build a greenfield production unit. It tackled the problems of bulk mixing and storage by installing instead multiple small mixers. The extra costs were covered by eliminating much of the storage and material handling equipment from the line. This also helped reduce the time spent on process cleandowns – there are fewer surfaces to clean and the smaller mixers run for longer. Rigorous analysis of set-up times resulted in immediate reductions of 65%. Recording on video what happened when process losses occurred resulted in a 60% reduction in changeover related waste. Says Thornton: 'Contrary to expectations the major difficulties were not related to variable packaging material specifications and machine engineering but with operator training and maintenance.'

Further improvements in flexibility came from negotiating a pattern of shifts that varied in length according to the time of week. Hold-ups and wastage in the package department were reduced by dividing packaging into two kinds – display and transport. The latter – which added nothing to merchandising – was swiftly rationalised from 20 types to two (an ink-jet printer customised them at the end of the line).

The benefits, says Thornton, can be summarised as:

● Enhanced customer service.
● An ability to respond faster to demand.
● A fresher product at time of consumption.
● The virtual elimination of out-of-code returns.
● A net reduction in capital charges.
● A much reduced chill store requirement.
● Lower quality costs through a reduction of process waste.
● Lower material handling costs.
● Simplified planning and logistics systems.

As in Japan, the 'purity' of UK companies' approaches to JIT varies widely. Richard Hickman, of Xerox Computer Services, argues strongly that partial JIT can meet many of a manufacturing company's objectives without the extensive disruption to existing ways of doing things that occurs with full-scale JIT. He explains:

Introduction of JIT as it is frequently presented requires a complete commitment of manufacturing strategy. Such a degree of commitment is not always available. This must not prevent individual managers from taking their own steps towards higher business productivity. Many factories would collapse under the strain of rapid transfer to JIT. These factories will go through an

*evolutionary period. Starting with their existing methods, pockets
of JIT implementations will be initiated. These pockets will expand
in size, so that all areas will eventually derive some benefits from
the JIT philosophy.*

Certainly, an initial focus on a specific problem seems in many cases
to provide the experience and understanding of JIT necessary to
embrace it wholeheartedly. For Cummins Engine, one such issue was
reducing machine set-up times. It had looked at conventional ways of
reducing set-ups in its Daventry plant, which averaged between 10
minutes and 90 minutes per machine. Investing £10000 in new
equipment, forecast the engineering staff, would cut set-up times by
21%. That total could be reduced by another 10% for a second tranche
of £10000. Thereafter, says Cummins, 'Things got tougher in
compliance with the law of diminishing returns – big money for small
improvements.'

Cummins brought in a JIT consultant to help it establish a no cost or
low cost approach that would have equal or greater impact on
reducing set-up times. It chose a pilot area – a cylinder block product
line already charged with delivering JIT to the assembly line – as a
pilot. It formed action teams (as opposed to study teams) and charged
them with the task of reducing set-up times by 50% within 6 months
and a further 25% within 12 months.

Cummins *did* spend money on this approach – but mostly on
training the production workers in what JIT meant, how to operate as
a team and how to record and analyse the information they would
need to make improvements. It also invested in video equipment to
record exactly what happened when set-up changes were made. The
teams of operators made and 'owned' the videos. They performed the
analyses to identify the elements of setting up that consumed most
time and looked for solutions with the aid of the plant engineers.

The results of this programme exceeded management's expectations. Says the company:

*The very first team to be formed had, within weeks of its inception,
reduced the set-up duration on a £500 000 machine which drills
and reams the cylinder head bolt holes on the cylinder block from
over 17 minutes to just 8 seconds for an outlay of £82. As an added
bonus (and unforeseen at the outset) the work done by this team on
their 'own' machine totally eliminated set-up on five other
machines, and partially reduced set-up on a further five machines
elsewhere in the production line. This was attained by a small
alteration to the product, which itself cost nothing to install, but
yielded a direct labour reduction of several thousand pounds
annually.*

*This kind of success, so early in the process, generated
enthusiasm and competition in subsequent teams – so much so*

that informal teams began to emerge spontaneously and start work ahead of the formal training schedule.

Overall, the teams exceeded their brief. Set times fell by 80% across the cylinder block production area. At the same time, the JIT programme as a whole received a substantial impetus. Says Cummins:

The achievement of the teams on the cylinder block line specifically, enabled batch sizes of the 12-cylinder and 16-cylinder product to be reduced to less than one third of their previous size (from 20–25 to around the 6–7 level, independent of product mix demand). This has led to shortened lead times, increased responsiveness, flexibility to meet short lead time mix changes and reductions to expensive inventory holdings.

A number of companies, among them IBM and Hewlett-Packard, who have already developed JIT internally, have moved to follow this up, by developing closer links with their supplier. IBM, for example, now has several suppliers, which are capable of delivering in a JIT mode and which have implemented JIT production.

JIT in UK subsidiaries of Japanese companies

Another study by Warwick University looked at a sample of manufacturing companies with Japanese parents. These companies fell into two quite specific categories. First, there was an existing company that had been taken over by a Japanese firm, and second, three Japanese companies that had set up on greenfield sites. As might be expected, the way in which JIT has been applied or is being prepared for, differs considerably between them.

Some of the most significant lessons about the differences in approach between UK and Japanese management came from the case of Sumitomo Rubber, which took over the ailing tyre manufacturing divisions of Dunlop in 1984. Sumitomo appointed a Japanese production director to take charge of the factory. The former production director worked alongside him during the first 2½ years. In preparing for JIT in the UK, top management concentrated on:

● *Housekeeping.* The implementation of JIT was led off by housekeeping. The Japanese production director immediately photographed the shopfloor as part of a 'before' and 'after' sequence. The employees do all the cleaning and tidying themselves. Sumitomo's attitude was 'If you are going to produce quality, you must start with a clean and tidy environment.'
● *Elimination of waste.*
● *Management of detail.* The Japanese management focused at a

greater level of detail than the previous UK management. This was one of the strongest contrasts between the two approaches to manufacturing technology.

● *Teamwork development.*

● *Investment in new plant and machinery.* Hitherto, the company had had very little investment in new plant – another painfully obvious indictment of the UK approach. The Japanese argued that this had led to the following negative cycle: Low investment–low enthusiasm–low quality–poor activity–no profit–again no investment.

The Japanese immediately began a programme of investment to bring the plant and machinery up to the standard of the Japanese plants. Nonetheless, say the current managers:

The £40 million investment by Sumitomo has mostly been spent on renovating and replacing old equipment. But that isn't the main reason for our increases in productivity. All of our three remaining factories are all doing equally well, although some had next to no money spent on their equipment. We've impressed the Japanese with the speed we have installed new equipment and changed production configurations. Last year we relocated 70 presses, but still met our production targets. The Japanese couldn't believe it.

● *Total preventive maintenance.* An early objective was to have 'good maintenance and good working of machinery'. For example, the maintenance engineers were taken off shifts and the operatives were trained and made more responsible for their machinery.

● *Statistical process control.* Around 500 people were trained in SPC at Fort Dunlop and 300 at Washington. Many of them could not even do decimals beforehand. Now they are totally in control of their machines.

● *Training.* Explains personnel director Ian Sloss:
Training has become a normal, day to day activity. Every employee has been to at least one course in the past year. Next year we will hold three times as many courses. Yet we only have one full time, professional trainer. All the rest of the teaching is done by the managers themselves. The person who is doing the teaching learns a lot. He has to put in extra hours to hold down his job and be a tutor.

● *Changing the production orientation.* Although the original UK production director was retained, there was a change in production managers overall. People with detailed knowledge of the production process and technology were promoted to managers. They replaced the old-style managers who saw themselves as separate from the technical function.

● *Development of flow in manufacturing.* This was the core of getting JIT into the company. The necessary actions included:

- ●Moving to a more flow-oriented layout.
- ●Investment in materials handling.
- ● Moving machines from functional grouping to be part of the flow.
- ● *Better quality components and material.* One reason for better materials handling was to reduce manual handling, and so minimise the chance of damage or picking up dirt.
- ● *Detailed performance objectives and continuous improvement.* The company had a set of non-financial performance measures that were used in Japan. These were related to productivity, waste and energy usage. (These measures had been developed by Dunlop years before, when Sumitomo Rubber was a partial subsidiary and transferred to Japan many years ago. The UK company had ceased to use and refine them.) These measures were broken down into targets at a very detailed level. Every group in the company was expected to meet these targets and to improve on them continuously.
- ● *Organisation.* The company had been organised around a series of profit centres, but the Japanese had reversed this and had moved to the concept of a single manufacturing team.

These actions (or the groundwork) were treated as essential precursors to the successful application of JIT.

Since then, the company has continued to progress both in each of these areas and in increasing flexibility. Important factors here have been the guarantee of job security given to the employees and a stress on employee involvement.

Says Sloss:

We now move people from one department to another with ease. There is no threat to their jobs; only the chance to add to their profit share. Currently, we are trying to give the engineering workers additional skills. We scrapped the shift system, putting them onto days and introducing planned maintenance to make sure the machines kept running. As a result, we have now reduced unplanned breakdowns from 11% to 1%.

We have pursued an almost fanatical insistence on improved communications. All managers have to be seen talking to their people, keeping in constant contact with them, holding discussion groups, encouraging quality circles and suggestion schemes. We have a regular monthly conference with all 40 key managers, to tell them about sales, profits, profit shares and other issues. This information is cascaded down the line during the week.

We have removed as many barriers between people as possible. We talk about 4-way communications (up, down and sideways). Everyone wears the same uniforms, including the managing director. We've also encouraged the different functions to come together. Sales people go into the factories. So do customers. And people in the factories go to meet the customers on their premises.

Anything that is devisive has to be removed. For example, last week we brought all cars on site because those left outside were being vandalised. We've got the space now.

When I came in 1979, we had seven canteens. Now we have one and the rest are all training rooms. The only difference between people is money.

The greenfield sites chosen for the Warwick research were of three contrasting types:

- Video-tape manufacture – high volume, make to stock.
- Photocopies – medium volume, make to programme/stock.
- Machine tools – low volume, make to order.

They exhibited four major common factors in their approach to implementing JIT, as follows.

Groundwork. Unlike the UK takeover company, the groundwork, although done thoroughly, was not seen as a major issue. The Japanese intended to build in from the start all the necessary practices and attitudes. This was accomplished by a number of measures including recruitment policies, training and sending key personnel to Japan. They seemed to focus, in particular, on the group leaders and the key technical personnel.

Plant. All three of the greenfield site companies had plant laid out for flow and had made adjustments in the way the plant was designed, to fit the UK environment. For instance, the video-tape manufacturer's Japanese plant was fully integrated with materials entering one end, with no buffer stocks at any point. For the UK, it was decided to keep the same level of automation, but to build in three small buffers. The reason was that, to maintain a highly integrated plant, there was a need for very low levels of machine downtime and very fast reaction to any problem. This, in turn, required the appropriate sort of personnel, including a very high level of skill. As the company felt that it would not get this sort of skill level in the short term, building a fully integrated plant would be too risky, and the small buffers were built in.

The photocopying company's Japanese plant was highly integrated in terms of materials handling and warehousing, whereas the UK plant was fairly simple without sophisticated materials handling. This difference seemed to be due mainly to the smaller scale of production.

The machine-tool manufacturing company's UK plant was as automated as its Japanese parents. It believed that its quality capability, in terms of the tolerances of the machines, was far higher than the company's Japanese plants. This was because of the UK's poor reputation for quality. Machines produced in the UK had to have higher quality to be able to overcome customer resistance to compete on an equal footing with machines produced in other countries.

Production scheduling. All three companies were reliant on the import of sets or kits of key components from their Japanese parent company. These kits required a long lead time for ordering and transportation. As a result, there would be between 2 and 4 months of kits in the pipeline. This shaped in a major way the practice of JIT in each company. Their ability to react to local marketplace demand was constrained by this long lead time. In addition, the foreknowledge of what was in the kits allowed companies to set stable production programmes well in advance. The way in which this stability was used and the way in which demand was met within a JIT environment varied from company to company. All three companies tried to keep level production schedules in the context of fluctuating demand and long lead times from Japan. The three companies chose to hold buffer stock in different ways; either in part processed stocks, one used finished goods. One used in-process stocks, one used finished goods stock, and the final company split the buffering between parts and finished goods. These policies are consistent with those that would be expected with the type of process and the type of demand satisfaction policies of each company. Unlike many UK companies, the policies on how and where to buffer and where to have stability were explicit.

Sourcing. They found this a particular barrier to implementing JIT in the UK. Failure to develop local sourcing will have a negative effect on UK suppliers and on the balance of payments performance of Japanese manufacturers who are forced to have a substantial import content. All three of the greenfield site companies had started with a high import content and positive intentions to increase considerably the local content. It was clear that this was by far the most difficult managerial task they faced. All complained of the difficulty of finding suitable suppliers, and between them listed a litany of problems, including supplier attitudes, inadequate quality, and an unwillingness to give service.

None of the companies solved this problem. When one company found a reliable supplier, all the other Japanese companies in the area were told. For example, an Edinburgh packaging company supplies a large number of Japanese companies in the Midlands, as it has the reputation of knowing how to handle the Japanese.

The pattern of purchasing practice of Japanese companies in the UK included:

● *Sourcing policies*. Dual sourcing is done in Japan in order to promote competition. Often the outcome in the UK was single-sourcing because of the inability to find a second source.

● *Regular delivery at specified times, usually at a longer interval than Japan*. Whereas hourly delivery is requested in Japan, daily delivery is requested in the UK.

● *Supplier development*. Working with suppliers to improve their ability to meet quality, technical requirements, price and delivery.

● *Joint technical development*. One company strongly preferred this. Where development was done jointly, the quality and technical aspects were good. Where standard items (for example, fastenings) were purchased, as the general UK industry standard was below that required by the Japanese, the company felt that it lacked sufficient leverage to raise industry-standard products.

● *Good communications of forward schedules*. For example, the photocopier assembler gave suppliers a six-month forecast, a three-month plan, and a one-month firm schedule. They then expected delivery twice a day.

● *Technical specification*. In contrast to Japan, where loose specifications are given to suppliers, the Japanese companies in the UK tended to give very tight specifications.

As with plant investment, the pattern in sourcing is one of adapting the Japanese practices to fit the UK environment.

The Japanese managers had some enlightening comments to make on their impressions of the British manager and his implementatiion of JIT. As one Japanese manager said: 'No manufacturing management practice is non-transferable, the issue is the degree of difficulty in transferring the practice.'

One critical observation the Japanese managers had to make was that less successful implementers of JIT often tend to ignore the lessons learned by Japan and focus on difficult techniques of JIT, without making sure that the groundwork is done first. The Kanban system is a good example. Three of the companies in the Warwick study had used Kanban in Japan, and felt that it could be introduced in the UK. However, as it is one of the most difficult of tools to implement, it was very low down on the list of things to implement. Similar considerations applied to quality circles, eliminating goods inward inspection and other JIT approaches.

The problems of JIT in the UK

Whilst there are many examples of good JIT implementation in the UK, there are even more companies with confused ideas and implementation. As with the western world in general, surveys of manufacturing companies indicate a number of common misconceptions about JIT. UK managers are particularly likely to see it in narrov terms as a set of techniques rather than a broad concept embracing many interrelated activities.

JIT is often inaccurately:

- *Equated directly with Kanban.* JIT has often been called 'the Kanban system'. However, Kanban is only part of JIT and starting a JIT programme with Kanban frequently leads to disappointment, because other fundamentals need to be tackled first.
- *Seen as starting with JIT purchasing.* Many companies, having seen other organisations successfully implement JIT purchasing, try to start JIT with purchasing. However, without attention to the full application of JIT internally, this approach will just pass inventories on to suppliers.
- *Seen as requiring single sourcing.* As described in Chapter 2, single sourcing is not the norm in Japan. All too often it is confused with working closely with the suppliers (which *is* practised in Japan).
- *Seen as aiming at batches of one.* One objective of JIT is to produce what is required, when it is required. This does not necessarily mean producing in batches of one, even if that is possible.
- *Regarded as an inventory reduction programme.* The most visible benefit of JIT is usually reduction of WIP. This leads many to see JIT as an inventory reduction programme. However, taking such a narrow perspective means that managers tend to neglect the broad based activities of JIT and the programmes may fail as a consequence.
- *Treated as an alternative to automation.* As pointed out in Chapter 2, Japanese manufacturing strategies treat JIT and automation as a partnership not as alternatives.

All of these misconceptions and confused ideas tend to reinforce existing barriers to effective implementation of JIT. Among the most common of these barriers are:

- *Tokenism.* JIT is the latest buzzword, therefore top managers push their managers to adopt it, with little thought as to the detail of what JIT is, or how appropriate it is.
- *Difficulty in knowing what to adopt and where to start.* This seems to derive from the lack of understanding described above.
- *The wrong starting point.* UK companies often want to start with a visible technique. As a result, they fail to do any of the necessary groundwork. This research indicates that this groundwork is essential for JIT implementation. A particularly common approach is to demand JIT delivery from suppliers as the first step in JIT introduction.
- *Blind following of prophets.* There are, as with many new management techniques, a number of 'gurus'. Managers often try to adopt some or all the techniques put forward with scant

attention to their order or even their relevance. In particular, the most visible techniques of JIT are those that differ most from Western practices, such as Kanban and quality circles. These are often the ones to be introduced first by UK companies and last by their Japanese counterparts.

● *Supply chain problems*. As mentioned above, many UK companies try to introduce JIT purchasing at an early stage. They, along with Japanese companies, soon find that unreliable suppliers make it difficult. However, unlike the Japanese, UK companies usually fail to do the necessary groundwork that such a quality certification, or provision to suppliers of long-term stable schedules, requires. Few would normally consider the option taken by Nissan to tie in suppliers more closely to its needs. It has moved some of them physically next to its Washington plant, acquiring additional land for the purpose. Other non-Japanese manufacturers, including Ford, are following suit to a greater or lesser degree.

Above all, many UK companies expect to see a fast, technique-led introduction, without bothering with any of the groundwork. As a Japanese production director commented: 'The process of introduction of JIT must be a long one of accumulation of good habits where it becomes possible to incorporate JIT. If, for example, you go over to the system overnight, I expect that it is impossible.'

JIT purchasing: Case examples

Toshiba Consumer Products

Toshiba Consumer Products (TCP) is based in Plymouth, UK, manufacturing colour television receivers, video cassette recorders and microwave ovens. It has three main sources of component supply – the parent company in Japan, other Far East vendors, and local (UK and Continental European) suppliers. The production lead time from starting to plan to actual production is 4 months, but TCP is working towards bringing it closer to the Japanese parent's current 2.5 months (targeted to fall to just 2 months).

TCP applies the same basic principles to its suppliers as does Toshiba Japan. Among them:

● We will not change our orders.
● We will pay on time as long as parts are delivered on time.
● We will pay correctly if parts are of good quality.

Implicit in this approach is that TCP will not inspect goods inward for quality or exact number – it assumes that the supplier has done so – and that it should not have to chase up suppliers for late orders. At first, this trust was misplaced, so TCP carried out an exercise to identify the problems. It analysed 1.5 million components for quality and accuracy of delivery and found, says materials director Peter Bayliss:

- Far East suppliers were far more accurate than local suppliers.
- If there was any tendency to supply incorrect quantities, then our Far East suppliers erred on the high side, whereas local suppliers' errors were equally spread about the required quantity.

To put pressure on the poorer performers, TCP prepared a league table on each issue and showed suppliers where they came in the league. This provided a meaningful basis for discussion on how performance could be improved. At least one company was able to expand its own customer base as a result of making the necessary improvements to give TCP the consistency of delivery it required.

To maintain the impetus for improvement, TCP started a number of initiatives. One was to establish a parts per million process to measure supplier performance and constantly to improve the level of performance required. TCP rejected the traditional European approach of setting a basic level of quality that must be achieved, on the grounds that it provided no real incentive for constant improvement.

Another initiative emphasised TCP's commitment to long-term relationships with suppliers. (Bayliss believes that the common practice of deliberately changing 5% of suppliers each year is both wasteful and damaging.) Every other year the company holds a suppliers' conference, 'to let them see our factory, reinforce our fundamental principles, and give an insight into the future'. Toshiba Japan has a suppliers co-operation group, with which it meets three or four times a year to discuss problems and invite help in devising a mutual solution.

In creating long-term relationships with suppliers, Bayliss believes it is important to ensure that there is good understanding between both parties at all levels. That has to include managing director to managing director; salesman to buyer; production controller to production controller; and so on, wherever there is an interaction in the logistics chain.

One of the benefits of this kind of relationship is that discussions between supplier and customer can often focus on cost *reductions* rather than cost increases. 'We expect,' says Bayliss, 'like other Japanese manufacturers, to receive a cost reduction at least once and, if possible, twice a year.' Interestingly, 'local' suppliers achieved greater cost reductions than Far Eastern suppliers in 1985 – an encouraging sign.

For TCP to implement JIT fully, it would have to reduce drastically the volume of Far Eastern parts. The logistics of shipping half-way around the world mean that arrival times can never be predicted with sufficient accuracy. However, many local vendors do deliver on a JIT basis – for example, packaging suppliers deliver twice daily.

One problem with local suppliers that Bayliss makes particular reference to is the practice of assigning 'allocations' to customers when the vendor experiences a major disruption to production. Because there is no buffer stock to speak of, such behaviour is not acceptable and TCP has had to engage in tough talking with some suppliers until the message got across.

Caterpillar UK*

Caterpillar has been in the UK since the 1950s and is based just outside Leicester. In the UK the company manufactures forklift trucks and backhoe loaders. No fabrication is carried out at all at the Leicester plant: it is assembly only. This naturally makes the plant very dependent on its suppliers. Any manufacturing philosophy or approach that enables a company to cement a closer and more reliable relationship with its suppliers had to, therefore, be of great interest to Caterpillar. It is thus not surprising that, in terms of the group's European operations, the Caterpillar UK plant has taken a lead in implementing JIT.

The need for JIT

The company as a whole is highly committed to JIT manufacturing and the UK initiative was a natural progression of this corporate thrust. The policy was fuelled by the slow and painful discovery of inventory costs which became particularly acute in the early 1980s when the company was faced with a down-turn in business. The company needed to generate extra cash and free up money that was snared in inventory; it decided to migrate to a philosophy of having inventory available only as and when needed.

The UK plant was very well placed to start work on implementing JIT for two basic reasons. Firstly, as mentioned above, there was no fabrication as such at Leicester. Unlike the US and continental European plants, which do much of their own fabrication, the Leicester plant assembles only, and buys in all its parts from outside suppliers. Having no machining centres and manufacturing processes to consider, this made the introduction of JIT at Caterpillar UK a relatively straightforward prospect.

Secondly, it was a particularly auspicious time for the UK plant to be making such major changes to the production process since it was in the process of introducing a new product line. This gave the Leicester plant the opportunity from the very start to engineer a new model range that would suit JIT-type production techniques.

While the plant had determined to push down its stocks it also intended to enhance its supplier relationships in the process. Caterpillar UK did not, therefore, aim to thrust its inventory down to

*Advanced Manufacturing Philosophies, Yankee Group Europe, 1988. Reproduced by permission of the Yankee Group Europe and Caterpillar (UK) Limited.

these suppliers. The company realised that this would have served no purpose since ultimately increased costs for the suppliers must lead to increased costs for Caterpillar.

Caterpillar UK has two main product lines: the forklift trucks, which have been made in Leicester for some time, and the backhoe loaders, which represent the new product range described above. Correspondingly, JIT is at the moment being applied primarily to the backhoe loaders, although the next stage of the project is to extend this further to the forklift trucks.

There are 15 basic model-types for the forklift trucks and only six for the backhoe loaders. More importantly still, the forklifts have 900 possible attachments (the Caterpillar term for 'options') while for the backhoe loader this is just 100.

Top management at Leicester first started planning for JIT between 1983 and 1984. Implementation began during 1984/5, and the plant recently marked shipment of its 10 000th unit under JIT.

When it was decided to go ahead with JIT in the UK, a project team was accordingly established, consisting of the respective managers concerned with purchasing, quality control, engineering, planning and manufacturing. The purchasing manager was the project leader, and he had a direct interface with the complementary team working on JIT in the US.

The company admits that the process of bringing people to work together more closely was not an easy one at any level, whether that be shopfloor or management. However, once the arguments of JIT had been recognised, the commitment began to grow.

Supplier relationships

The fulcrum on which the success or failure of the JIT initiative rested was that of supplier acceptance. Indeed, Caterpillar intrinsically recognised this fact by appointing the purchasing manager as co-ordinator of the project. But supplier acceptance alone was not enough. Since Caterpillar itself did no fabrication, much of the burden of future investment would inevitably be passed down to those that did manufacture: the suppliers. Caterpillar's suppliers, therefore, had to be persuaded that it was in their interests too to migrate towards JIT principles.

Before JIT could be implemented, Caterpillar had to overcome the natural fears of its suppliers about the possible consequences of JIT. The company found that there were in fact two main anxieties. Firstly, the suppliers feared that if there was no storage on the line at Caterpillar, they themselves would have to store up extra inventory.

Secondly, the suppliers feared that they would be expected to start delivering 1 day's supply of parts each day. The planning mechanism Caterpillar devised to support JIT, therefore, had to be able to provide suppliers with some basis for predicting likely demand for parts and a specific horizon during which time orders would not be changed. The system that Caterpillar eventually developed is discussed in the next section.

In practice, some stores are still kept at Caterpillar of between 1 and 5 days. Exactly which parts will be stored and for how long is decided on an individual basis depending on the supplier concerned, the nature of the part, distance, transport costs and so on.

Caterpillar could not hope to develop JIT-type relationships with all its suppliers, so the company instituted a programme to limit its supplier base. During 1987, the plant reduced its suppliers by 20%. This process is still going on and has become more important in the context of plans to implement EDI over the following years.

With those suppliers that are left, Caterpillar has tried to develop a closer relationship. There are long-term agreements with some of these suppliers. The company does not, however, offer a guaranteed volume of orders. At the same time, although Caterpillar wanted to encourage the suppliers to accept JIT, it was careful not to give too much away.

The supplier/customer relationship may be closer, but it still has to be carefully documented and defined, particularly in terms of mutual responsibilities. JIT effectively gives the supplier a greater stake in the success of its customers' businesses, but it also leaves the latter more open to harm in the event of mistakes. Thus it is very important, says Caterpillar, for instance, to make sure the supplier is responsible for delivering the material. This issue of defining responsibility becomes especially critical with respect to quality control (discussed below).

All Caterpillar's high-value or high-volume suppliers are working on a JIT basis. In absolute terms a large number of suppliers are still functioning in the traditional way, but for Caterpillar the 15% of suppliers that are functioning on a JIT basis represents about 80% of the purchases. Altogether the plant has about 30 suppliers working JIT.

The difficulties of coaxing suppliers into the closer relationships demanded by JIT are well documented. However, there are difficulties for the 'instigator' too, in this case Caterpillar, in adjusting to the new regimen. In order to get closer to its suppliers and bring about the smaller, more frequent deliveries, Caterpillar has itself had to become a lot more open with and trusting of its suppliers. The information that Caterpillar sends to these suppliers is based on sales forecasts and orders, which it uses itself internally. This information was formerly company confidential.

The quality issue

Quality is a vital issue for any organisation working along JIT principles where, by definition, there is no tolerance of wastage. Inevitably also the momentum for quality assurance and quality control procedures is pushed further and further down the supply chain. Thus, while Caterpillar forces more responsibility on to its suppliers, these suppliers will themselves force similar demands upon their suppliers, and so on. Caterpillar has tried to formalise quality control procedures at a number of levels both at its own front door and before the goods leave the suppliers' premises.

The first level is built into the supplier/client relationship via a prequalification procedure. Before it can be considered for supplier status under JIT, a company has to document its inspection procedures and produce a quality plan. Only when this has been done can the supplier be considered for the job.

The second level of quality control is at the Caterpillar plant itself where a team of quality engineers works together with the buyers. When the buyers and quality engineers find a problem they decide on a course of action.

A third level of quality control is carried out by a group of roving quality analysts who visit suppliers checking, not the quality of parts themselves, but that the proper quality procedures, in other words the quality plan, are being followed.

Finally, by way of incentive to suppliers, rather than a specific check as such, Caterpillar makes an annual award, or as the company calls it, a supplier certification award. This is made 12 months after the introduction of the quality plan to those suppliers that have maintained a record of high-quality parts. A plaque is presented to the company at a special ceremony.

The JIT mechanism

Caterpillar works on a build-to-order basis, a system that was in place prior to implementation of JIT. It builds only what it can sell and has very little finished goods stores. The company has retained its existing MRP II system and is using it in connection with both JIT and non-JIT production. The system is quite an old one that Caterpillar designed itself. It produces a monthly planning forecast for the next 10 months which is circulated to suppliers. Suppliers not working on JIT principles continue, as in the past, to use these monthly forecasts as a delivery schedule. The JIT suppliers, on the other hand, use them for general planning purposes only.

Delivery schedules for JIT suppliers are issued weekly on the basis of actual orders received by Caterpillar. The documentation the supplier receives is thus the actual daily order log by part number spread over a 25-day horizon. Since the suppliers need to have a minimum period of fixed orders on which to plan, a 25-day (i.e. 5 weeks) fixed planning horizon was agreed upon. The company hopes that implementation of electronic data interchange (EDI) will eventually enable it to reduce this to 20 days. The MRP II schedules and the weekly order log should be broadly in line – they should confirm each other.

To date, Caterpillar UK has implemented JIT independently of EDI. The company has only recently started to put EDI in place, so for the present, drivers continue to pick up orders and documentation upon delivery of parts. In terms of getting the parts from the supplier and into the plant, however, Caterpillar has made some major changes.

Instead of having one receiving area for all deliveries, Caterpillar is arranging for major pieces to be delivered to and unloaded at the place where they will be used. This has already started to happen but is not easy to achieve. In the first place, the company has had to put extra doors into the factory to facilitate the additional access.

Another question centred on how the goods would henceforth be logged into the plant. Caterpillar has solved this by posting a receiving employee at the factory gates who will take the delivery note from the driver. The receiving employee will punch the delivery information into the computer which responds with a direction to the appropriate reception point for each delivery.

Another result of delivering parts directly to the relevant line has been to decrease the importance of counting them. If the parts are received close to their assembly point, it is no longer necessary to keep track of the individual pieces. Caterpillar uses the two-box system, which is similar to Kanban. The worker has two bins; when he has used up one, then he pushes it out of the way and takes the second. The first bin is then empty and waiting to be filled. The boxes themselves act as a flag to signal the need for more parts in the factory.

People and attitudes

All the people that the Yankee Group Europe spoke to at Caterpillar had similar comments to make about the changes in their jobs that resulted from JIT. At the managerial level, the general comment was that the nature of the actual job had not changed but, firstly, it was necessary to interface with many more people, and secondly, everything happened a lot faster. Speed, of course, is a doubleedged sword.

On the shopfloor, it was found that supervisors had to be much more vigilant and shopfloor workers in general began to carry more responsibility. Similarly there was noticeably more teamwork. People began to work better together, notably materials and production staff, and mistakes or problems were discovered more quickly.

The new integration and co-operation did not happen overnight, and the process is still going on. But one of the ways that Caterpillar fostered it was by involving the workforce from the very beginning in what was going on. The workforce was encouraged to put forward ideas and discuss them. This demanded a totally different management approach, which in its turn did not spring up immediately, but was learnt through trial and error.

The way in which additional responsibility has permeated the organisation is reflected in the fact that there is now, for instance, only one grade of assembler throughout the Leicester plant. This makes the assembler a much more flexible and highly skilled worker.

Staffing levels are gradually going down at Caterpillar, but this, the company argues, has not been the main thrust of its JIT policy. More important, says the company, is the wider and more responsible role that the existing people are being encouraged and expected to take on. The planning staff have been considerably upgraded as a result of introducing JIT. Caterpillar now takes graduates and trains them in the new methods.

Pros and cons

Caterpillar believes that its implementation of JIT principles has been very successful to date. The company has gone from an inventory cycle of about 2 months to less than 1 month. In other words, Caterpillar has increased its inventory turns from six to about 14. The company also believes that it has become more competitive because it is quicker on its toes and design changes can be implemented more swiftly. The plant is much more integrated and much more professional than before.

Lead time, which at Caterpillar is measured in terms of start time to ready-to-ship (RTS) has decreased and is still decreasing. The company now measures performance in terms of whether it meets the RTS to plan, i.e. the delivery date promised to customers.

Quality has improved even over the high level prior to JIT. There is a strong element of 'when everything is going well, it's going well', but by forcing people to be more professional and more responsive, many more problems ought to be avoidable than in the past. JIT has, for example, forced the planning engineers to do a better job and the logistics of flow have improved. However, it only takes one hitch to stop production.

Caterpillar admits that while JIT has undoubtedly enabled the company to become more competitive, at the same time, life with JIT is a little like living with a time bomb. There is always a nagging sense of insecurity. The company also, however, accepts this as part of the cost of JIT. One manager at Caterpillar noted that there was absolutely no doubt that life under the old manufacturing regime was a lot easier, and also a lot less profitable.

Despite the vast improvements in quality that have been made, the company still stresses quality control as one of the main areas where it wishes to see further improvements. The further towards 'total JIT' the company moves the more crucial quality will become.

Another area where Caterpillar is still trying to improve is in terms of the quality and accuracy of information that it has available both for its own use and for its suppliers. It is hoped that the EDI project will go some considerable way towards improving the information flow to and from suppliers.

In terms of data collection, Caterpillar is now grappling with the problem of how to introduce barcoding. This would greatly reduce the problem of knowing where parts are in the plant, and so on. At the moment a lot of counting is done manually, leaving plenty of opportunity for error. The ideal stage to apply the bar codes is before the parts even enter the plant, i.e. before they leave the suppliers, but Caterpillar has had some problems with this in terms of conflicting bar-code standards and systems of different vendors.

In summary, the advantages of JIT at Caterpillar have been:

- Reduced inventory.
- Higher quality.
- Improved efficiency and responsiveness.
- Reduced lead times.
- More integrated production.
- Improved teamwork.
- Improved planning.
- Greater individual responsibility.
- Closer and more reliable supplier relations.

The disadvantages of JIT have been:

- Increased dependence on suppliers.
- Underlying sense of insecurity.
- Vulnerability to outside disruptions.
- Increased pressure on workforce and management.

5. JIT in Europe

The diversity of European cultures has spearheaded a variety of approaches to implementing JIT. However, there are a number of fundamental problems common to all countries. In this chapter, we examine some of these problems through the eyes of a Japanese expert, and extract lessons from some successful implementations.

5 JIT in Europe

Overview

The pressures to improve manufacturing practices in Europe are much the same as those in the US and UK. So, too, are the major problems companies face in translating theory into practice. Some of the issues have been placed in context by Japan's Prof. Hajime Yamashina, who has studied manufacturing plants in Sweden, Finland and the Netherlands. Among his conclusions are:

- High labour costs compared with developing countries are forcing greater attention to productivity improvement. There is increasing awareness of the capability of JIT to increase productivity through, for example, eliminating wasteful movement (of both people and product) and through making employees multiskilled and in charge of multiple machines.
- The initial interest in JIT in firms in those countries tends to come from the materials departments rather than from production or from top management as an element of manufacturing strategy. Inevitably, this gives it a bias that may damage its chances of implementation across the organisation.
- European firms frequently find it difficult to appreciate the importance of good housekeeping as a precursor for an effective JIT programme.
- European companies are often better at analysing problems than resolving them. Although statistical process control techniques are now reasonably widely spread, the ability to follow through is less well developed. Says Yamashina: 'It is often the case that quality control people investigate problems through graphs and check-sheets and conjecture causes by results without investigating the actual spot. This approach costs time and involves unnecessary discussions. What is needed instead is quick, on the spot action for solving problems.'
- As in the West as a whole, manufacturing companies in the three countries studied had a very different workforce structure. The typical structure of the production workforce in Japan has fewer operators and more engineers. Part of this difference is the growth of 'specialists' in Western companies. According to Yamashina, not only do many specialists lack the broadness of knowledge that allows them to draw on other relevant specialisations, but also the depth of their knowledge is often inadequate.
- Organisation structure, too, was a limiting factor in the European companies. Explains Yamashina:

There seems to exist strong sectionalism between different departments in Western companies because of individualism. People tend to see problems only from the viewpoint of the company, and call them as specialists. Because of this sectionalism, many good improvement schemes must be abandoned. Improvement must be made without interfering in the interests of other departments. But, in many cases, improvement can be made by the cooperation with other sections and sometimes by sacrificing the interests of them. For example, implementation of the JIT production system increases transportation cost, but reduces other costs such as inventory cost, labour cost and space cost, and as a whole contributes to the reduction of production cost. If such is the case in Western countries, it becomes extremely difficult to carry out such a scheme or at least take a long time. The major obstacle to the implementation of JIT production system was not top management nor workers but middle-class managers due to their lack of overall view and sectionalism. Individuality has to give ground to company's needs at some point. Newly coming industrial products are getting more and more complicated and highly value added. To produce such products, it is vitally important to organise people effectively and make them cooperate with each other.

● European companies are more resistant to change than their Japanese counterparts. The difference can be seen in the two statements: 'If it ain't broke, don't fix it' and 'Make changes or you don't progress'.

A useful insight into how far European companies have embraced JIT and its associated techniques comes from a recent survey by A.T. Kearney.* The survey looked at the experiences of 500 companies and focused primarily on logistics (Fig. 5.1). Nearly two-thirds of the companies were at a fairly primitive level of logistics management – operating in crisis mode, using fragmented technical disciplines and less than a quarter have links with suppliers and customers and are incorporating logistics into their strategic planning as a means of gaining competitive advantage.

The survey asked the companies about their materials planning and control improvement activities and found that approximately one in five had made use of JIT or Kanban. Other relevant results are shown in Fig. 5.1.

A generally supporting view comes from Professor Horst Wildemann of the University of Passau. Many European companies, says Wildemann,** 'look at JIT in the same way as the seven blind men, who each felt one part of an elephant and tried to describe the whole of it.' Better, he advises, to 'approach it through a number of pilot projects that can then be integrated with each other. In other words, it is more a concept of learning by doing.' Companies that have been successful in introducing JIT in Germany, he observes, usually have a

---

*Logistics Productivity: the Competitive Edge in Europe, A.T. Kearney Inc., 222 South Riverside Plaza, Chicago, Illinois 60606, USA.

* *Just-in-Time Systems and Euro-Japanese Industrial Collaboration, edited by U. Holl and H. Trevor, Campus Verlag, Frankfurt, 1988.

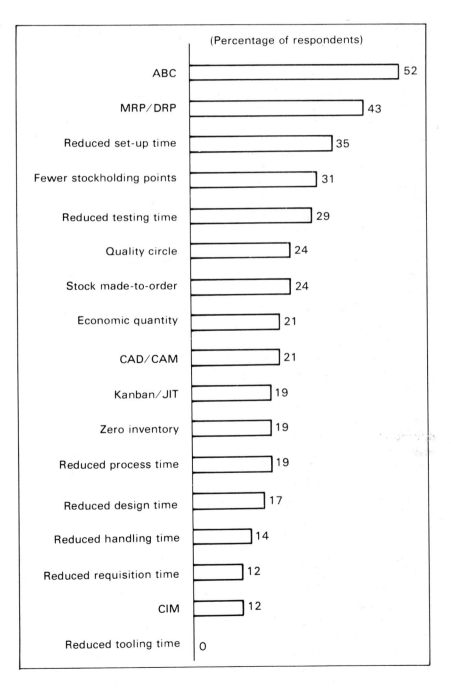

Fig. 5.1 Materials planning and control improvement actions (Source: A.T. Kearney, Inc.)

(Percentage of respondents)

ABC	52
MRP/DRP	43
Reduced set-up time	35
Fewer stockholding points	31
Reduced testing time	29
Quality circle	24
Stock made-to-order	24
Economic quantity	21
CAD/CAM	21
Kanban/JIT	19
Zero inventory	19
Reduced process time	19
Reduced design time	17
Reduced handling time	14
Reduced requisition time	12
CIM	12
Reduced tooling time	0

top management team expert both in understanding the processes and in implementing major change.

The problem with many companies, however, is that, while top management may accept that competitive advantages, middle management, which has to implement the JIT strategy, is often less enthusiastic because it has to make substantial changes in behaviour. On the other hand, JIT implementation in Germany is helped by other forces, among them a joint union/employer initiative to humanise work. Prime elements in this initiative are job enrichment, job rotation and increased training.

Wildemann also suggests that JIT is merely a stepping stone on a longer path. He explains: 'A simple transfer of this type of production system into a European setting can at best enable us to keep up with the conditions of competitiveness that some other competitors have already attained.' To regain competitive advantage, European companies must innovate and adopt JIT, to create the cash flow needed to invest in computer-aided manufacturing and flexible manufacturing systems.

To Dr-Ing. Wilhelm Gangelmeier of West Germany's Institute for Production Technology and Automation, the adoption of JIT techniques is a matter of survival for many German companies. The combination of high wages, high taxes and import competition in the domestic markets requires a strategy that can only be fulfilled through JIT techniques, he maintains.

The experience of European companies that have introduced JIT

As in the UK and the US, the range of companies which have adopted full-scale or partial JIT is large. As in Japan, the automobile industry has taken a vanguard position. Volkswagen is quoted as aiming to reduce the average production time for all models from 33 days to 15 days. At Daimler-Benz, vendor Keiper-Recaro deliver seat fittings direct to the assembly line by conveyor belt every 20 minutes. Among other companies that have become enthusiastic converts are Renault and Bendix Electronics in France, and Avon Cosmetics in West Germany.

Bendix Electronics produces electronic systems for the automotive industry, in three plants approximately 100 km apart. The company needed to reduce lead-time. It recognised five priority actions necessary to succeed in doing so, says Francis Peyronnet,* manager of Kanban and production control. These were:

---

*Improving work flow in the shop: MRP Kanban integration, by F. Peyronnet, Bendix Electronics, France, *Proceedings 3rd International Conference on Just-in-Time Manufacturing*, IFS Publications, Bedford, 1988.

- To decrease and even eliminate stocks of raw materials and finished products, as they are expensive to store and do not always meet the customer requirements.
- To reduce manufacturing in-process level, which is not very homogeneous (you do not always achieve a good product at a good time), and which generates indirect costs (you have to schedule several levels of bill of materials, and sometimes to manage emergency stocks of semi-finished products).
- To minimise risks involved by obsolescent products, by reducing changes, and by meeting exactly requirements.
- To make production equipment flexible, by creating technical task forces that will think about the eventual means necessary to reduce set-up times, or to modify manufacturing products.
- To make employees versatile by investing in training of each operator.

The first Kanban lines were launched in May 1985 and these were rapidly extended until, by mid-1988, 180 products and 380 subassemblies were being produced using JIT. Bendix's system uses MRP for long- and medium-term schedules; Kanban for workshop planning. Part of the Kanban process involves making the operators aware of the latest time the customer line can take delivery of the subassembled component. Another important element is a visible display that warns both Kanban users and their supervisor when a bottleneck is developing. This display is also valuable to production management, who can see immediately the state of production flow, without reference to graphs or complicated charts. However, the information is aimed primarily at the operators, who are responsible for the organisation and quality of their work. Says Peyronnet: 'They are personally in charge of cards and product flows and of starting their production in accordance with the information they have.'

Among the benefits recorded by Bendix are:

- 30% reduction of in-process parts and stabilisation of the number of parts in process between preset maximum and minimum levels.
- Better workflow between departments, with deliveries from the manufacturing operators now taking place four times a day.
- Less indirect work (e.g. fewer warehousemen looking for parts and fewer production control staff working out schedules).

Avon Cosmetics' West German subsidiary distributes up to 300 000 products a day to 100 000 representatives around the country. Since 1982 it has concentrated on developing JIT with the aim of resolving some of the conflicts inherent in any business that requires immediate delivery of multiple small units to a large number of outlets. The prime conflicts, as expressed by the company, are:*

*Just-in-time manufacturing – effects on costs and logistics, by M. Schumann, Avon Cosmetics, Germany, *Proceedings 3rd Internatiional Conference on Just-in-Time Manufacturing*, IFS Publications, Bedford, 1988.

● Low capital investment versus high readiness to deliver.
● Short throughput times versus full utilisation of factory capacity.
● Low inventories versus 100% product availability.

Avon's JIT programme had to take account of the pattern of selling, which is built around 18 campaigns each year. Avon representatives send orders in to a central point and expect to receive the goods within 6 days.

One of the first actions Avon took was to improve the accuracy of sales estimates, by piloting each campaign with 2% of its representatives, 3 weeks ahead. This cut the gap between real and estimated demand from 33% to 14%. This is sufficient to ease the most severe problems of materials supply and production scheduling.

A second step was to rationalise production so that each of the company's European factories had its own product specialisations. In some ways, this went against the spirit of JIT, in that it achieved reduced set-up times by increasing the average run size. Considerable investment went into training and into supplier education. Suppliers now receive 9-month contracts under which they either work JIT themselves, or maintain a stock 50% above predicted demand. All vendors are 'approved' and the best for quality and reliability receive awards presented at the Avon factory.

Avon's production and delivery system is not true JIT, in that it does not manufacture to meet each representative's order. But it is a good example of the application of JIT techniques to a difficult market sector, and the pay-offs, though less spectacular than in companies which have gone the whole hog in JIT implementation, follow a familiar pattern. Some of the principal benefits measured between 1982 and 1987 are shown in Table 5.1.

Table 5.1   How Avon improved performance with a JIT approach

	1982	1987
Inventory values		
Finished goods	100%	75%
Components	100%	47%
Raw ingredients	100%	48%
Costs of warehousing and handling	100%	75%
Average run size	100%	82%
Readiness to delivery (customer service)	94.0%	99.7%
Quality		
Materials	91.5%	97.7%
Production	98.4%	99.7%
Commissioning	1:3000	1:15000

Case examples

Andreas Stihl KG*

Andreas Stihl KG is a West German manufacturer of power saws and similar equipment, exporting 90% of its sales. JIT came to the company as a part of a logical procession of rationalisations, which culminated in setting up an autonomous materials control system, responsible for the flow of materials from procurement to product despatch. JIT at Andreas Stihl covers:

- Purchasing.
- Production.
- Distribution and warehousing.
- Product development.

In introducing JIT, the company first set about a comprehensive education programme, aimed at telling everyone who would be affected by the changes what was going to happen, why and what the implications for their jobs and roles in the company would be. It then embarked on a massive training programme to increase the range and level of skills of those employees. The trade union (IG Metall) was co-operative, not least because of a wages deal that paid operators according to their skill level rather than the particular work they were doing.

Chairman Hans Peter Stihl is adamant that JIT must include all parts of the organisation. He draws the analogy of a convoy, which is limited to the speed of its slowest member. But, he stresses, in 'establishing a JIT system – by which I mean an integrated, total system, starting with assembly and going right through to the market – one has to think in terms of a time span of 10 years.' A step-by-step process is therefore inevitable.

Among major improvements made so far is reduction of setting-up time in rail production. Automating the changeover of the heavy stamping tool that is the main process in producing rails and linking it to a computer-controlled warehouse that can deliver the appropriate raw materials (steel strip or coil) on call has reduced set-up times from 2 hours to 3 minutes. Two minutes after that, production can resume. At the same time, automation has improved the quality of the product. But the main benefits have come from greater production flexibility. Says Stihl: 'For instance, when we receive an electronically transmitted order from the USA for a few spare rails, we have the technology to make the rails 1 hour later and to send them the same day by air freight to the USA. The customer can get the spare part he needs on the following morning. Previously it was impossible to deal

*Just-in-Time Systems and Euro-Japanese Industrial Collaboration edited by U. Holl and M. Trevor, Campus Verlag, Frankfurt, 1988.

with small orders for spare parts because of the high cost of set-up time or changeover.'

A combination of JIT and quality have also made their impact in waste reduction. Says Stihl: 'The costs for scrap and reworking in the production of one very difficult part fell from 72% to just 16% of production wages. In money terms, this was a saving of DM 1 million. The saving in time was 42%, and the saving in inspection costs was 32%.'

Recognising the important role suppliers have in making the difference between success and failure in a JIT programme, Stihl early on set up regular suppliers' meetings, to examine issues of quality control. The aim was to eliminate the duplication of effort that occurs in inspecting goods both at the supplier's premises and at Stihl's goods inwards. Consistency was monitored carefully until each supplier could demonstrate an ability to supply at minimal defect levels over at least a 6-month period. Stihl also shared its plans with the suppliers and offered them 2- to 3-year contracts in return for their making the investments necessary in new skills and equipment. Eventually, Stihl hopes to insert around 120 components directly into the production process.

One of the keys to success, believes Hans Stihl, is spending time at the beginning discussing the implications and potential of JIT at top management level until there is a genuine consensus. 'Each area must stand behind this overall concept with complete conviction', he insists. Progress may be slow, but a sure sign that it is happening is when each area runs a pilot project and assumes responsibility for informing colleagues and dealing with their reservations, for training them, and finally for convincing them. 'Then', says Stihl, 'you can succeed in gaining full acceptance of the system down to the last operator.'

DAF Trucks

Dutch vehicle manufacturer DAF Trucks has been moving towards JIT for several years. The process, as seen by K. Van Eynde, DAF's manager, logistics systems, is illustrated below. Van Eynde describes the process as follows:

If DAF Trucks is to become a JIT company, a programme covering the whole company is required. The forces of the entire organisation will be mobilised [Fig. 5.2].

● The basic strategy should be:

○ *Simplify layout and process technology.*
○ *Reconsider product design.*
○ *Simultaneously provide training courses and instructions.*
○ *Subsequently select and use a control concept.*

Fig. 5.2 DAF Trucks in The Netherlands has mobilised the entire organisation in the drive for JIT

● *Make the presentation of instructions (both assembly operations or office procedures) more visual. Van Eynde advises using such common Japanese techniques as:*
  ○ *Instructions in the form of colour cartoons at the work stations.*
  ○ *Production progress shown on large light panels.*
  ○ *'Failure panels' to indicate whether any machines are out of order.*
  ○ *Showing the operator a bottleneck machine in a photograph.*
  ○ *Defining locations for packing units by lines on the floor.*
  ○ *Photographs on the outside of packing units to show what products are inside.*
● *Training courses will be useless if they are not followed up by mutual consultation and communication. Training and consultation should be integral parts of the same programme. The training module for the middle management should be made operational first. The middle management should be clearly shown the consequences of 'non-flow' and it should be trained in creativity. First of all, however, a consultative structure should be created.*

111

- *The fact that a product can or cannot be produced in flow should be a major consideration in the make/buy decision; in other words, a part which cannot be produced in flow by DAF, should be bought out. The supplier selected should, of course, show the required flexibility in supplying the products (delivery periods, changing of delivery periods, frequency of delivery, timely delivery). Examine the potential for reducing lead time for in-company production processes.*
- *Invest in preventive measures to ensure an acceptable level of quantitative reliability [Fig. 5.3]. The organisation should be set up in such a way that:*
  - *Inspections are integrated into the process.*
  - *Every department can guarantee a 100% reliability of its output.*
  - *Suppliers deliver the quantities specified and mark consignments with a 'quantity approved' label after inspection.*
- *The flow of stock, particularly in the assembly area is accelerated. A storage area in the flow of goods is the result of a conscious*

Fig. 5.3 Preventative measures have been adopted by DAF Trucks to ensure acceptable levels of reliability

choice. This element, too should be organised in such a way that the flow is not interrupted. DAF will have to invest large sums in the provision of storage and trans-shipment areas.

6. Implementation Strategies for JIT

A successful JIT programme starts with a clear positioning within an overall corporate strategy. Because it will precipitate fundamental changes in many areas of operation, rather than just in manufacturing, top management must be fully aware of the implications of JIT implementation and committed to the extensive personal effort required. This chapter starts by examining these issues, then proceeds to discuss the stages of preparation, selection of JIT techniques, how to involve the workforce, and creation of a JIT supply system. In effect, it is a practical guide for top management to follow in ensuring the viability of their JIT programme.

6 Implementation Strategies for JIT

Creating a JIT strategy

'The only period in the past 15 years that we dipped in productivity was the 6 months when we were introducing JIT', admits the chief executive of a large Japanese manufacturing group. One of the main reasons, he explains, is that the process required such a radical change in the normal way of doing things that management attention was diverted. Nonetheless, he is convinced that, without JIT, the company could not have sustained its consistently high annual productivity increases.

The lesson learnt by that company was that JIT cannot be introduced in a hurry. It must be a strategic exercise, with detailed preparation and planning. The major problems need to be foreseen, tested and overcome *before* implementation, because the little ones will require more than enough management attention on their own.

A useful starting point in determining where to focus efforts is to understand where the real costs and cost drivers of the business lie. This is easier said than done, because many of these costs will be hidden – for example, costs of non-compliance, and non-value-added activities. However, detailed analysis along the lines suggested in Fig. 6.1, by Andersen Consulting (formerly Arthur Andersen) will reveal where the greatest savings can be made.

Before creating a JIT strategy, top management will need to ask itself a number of key questions. Among them:

● How will JIT affect our marketplace?
● How suitable is JIT for our manufacturing environment?
● Should we invest in JIT, advanced manufacturing technology or both?
● What fundamental changes do we need to make, to turn our company into a JIT company?

Cost components / Cost drivers	Product design	Sourcing and logistics	Physical facilities	Organisation	
Basic					H
Cost of non-compliance					I
NVA activities					D
NVA investition					D
Downtime					E
Other					N
		Total cost			

Fig. 6.1 Cost cube
(Source: Andersen Consulting)

Taking these in turn:

How will JIT affect our marketplace?

Any company seriously considering its manufacturing strategy must start by considering the marketplace and competition. If your company is competing against the Japanese, it is competing against JIT. The JIT philosophy is now so widespread in Japan, that few exporting companies do not use all or some of the JIT approaches and techniques.

The benefits from JIT can be considered in terms of their market impact. For example, reduction in manufacturing lead time can lead to being able to compete on responsiveness in the marketplace. Fig. 6.2 lists the benefits (in rank order as reported in a Warwick University survey), and shows how these can lead to different forms of competitive advantage. The links can also be looked at from the reverse perspective. If a company has chosen its competitive strategy, it can match the strategy to the particular capabilities of JIT. Examples of how this can be done are shown in Fig. 6.3.

How suitable is JIT for our manufacturing environment?

The traditional view is that JIT is most suitable for a repetitive manufacturing environment, yet there is no clear definition of what repetitive manufacturing is. Companies usually define it as being manufacture of products that are regularly ordered. One UK company

JIT capability	Competitive advantage derived from JIT capability
1. WIP reduction	Lower cost manufacture Reduced order to delivery lead time
2. Increased flexibility	Responsive to customer demands: Volume Short lead time Product change
3. Raw materials reduction	Lower cost manufacture
4. Increased quality	Higher quality products Lower cost manufacture
5. Increased productivity	Lower cost manufacture
6. Reduced space requirements	Lower cost manufacture
7. Lower overheads	Lower cost manufacture

Fig. 6.2 JIT and competitive advantage

Fig. 6.3 Company strategies and JIT

Competitive strategy	JIT capability supporting strategy
Rapid response to customer needs	Flexibility WIP reduction
Compete on quality	Increased quality
Compete on price	WIP reduction Raw material reduction Increased productivity Reduced space requirements Lower overheads
Rapid product change	Flexibility

defines this as being any product that is ordered at least once per month by a customer, another as at least once a week. Using this definition, repetitive manufacture will embrace most flow and line manufacture, a surprisingly large proportion of batch manufacture but only a limited proportion of jobbing and projects. Methodologies are being developed (by Professor Bill Berry of the University of North Carolina) to determine for a batch manufacturing environment, whether all or part of a company's products are repetitive and hence suitable for JIT. Fig. 6.4 describes the four main forms of repetitive manufacture.

There are a number of industries where there is already a high degree of flow in manufacturing, such as food and drink, where companies are not sure whether JIT has anything to offer. These flow-based manufacturing environments can be considered as having a large proportion of the elements of JIT in place. However, in most cases they can still benefit by adopting selected JIT techniques. In particular, JIT purchasing and set-up time reduction can lead to major benefits in process industries.

At the other end of the spectrum, the nature of jobbing and projects makes them unsuitable for the flow elements that are the core of JIT. However, as with flow manufacture, selected JIT techniques can be suitable for these environments. These include set-up time reduction, total quality control and workforce flexibility.

The suitability of JIT for particular process environments is summarised in Fig. 6.5. The companies in the centre of the diagram

Family
Different families of parts, each with its own small line

Mixed
Mixed models made on a single line

Dedicated
Single model, single line

Flow
Flow process, chemical etc.

Fig. 6.4   Types of repetitive manufacture

Fig. 6.5 JIT and
the manufacturing
environment

Variety				
	Jobbing project			
High	Part of JIT unsuitable, application of selected techniques			
		Batch manufacture JIT suitable for part of plant		
			JIT suitable for all of plant	
Medium			*Line manufacture* JIT suitable for manufacture	
				Process manufacture
Low				Much of JIT in place, application of selected techniques
	Low	*Medium*		*High*
		Volume		

almost certainly have part or all of their manufacturing suitable for JIT; those at the top right and the bottom left will be suitable for selected applications.

A second means of determining whether JIT is appropriate is to examine the inherent complexity of product structure and process routing. The more complex these are, the less suitable JIT is for planning and controlling production. This is illustrated in Fig. 6.6. However, this is not a static relationship. One of the key elements of JIT is the reduction of complexity. Companies, which are in an environment unsuitable for JIT, can *make* it suitable by a programme of reduction of product and process complexity.

Should we invest in JIT, AMT or both?

It has been argued by a number of people, for example Ingersoll Engineers, that the route to automation is 'simplify, automate, integrate'. An increasing number of organisations are using JIT as the 'simplify' element in their automation strategies. There are a number of strong arguments that companies considering automation and Computer-Integrated-Manufacture should pursue JIT in advance of or in parallel to automation. First, some of the methodologies used for planning CIM are used in JIT, in particular group technology. Second, if a major JIT programme is conducted prior to automation, the simplification inherent in JIT may:

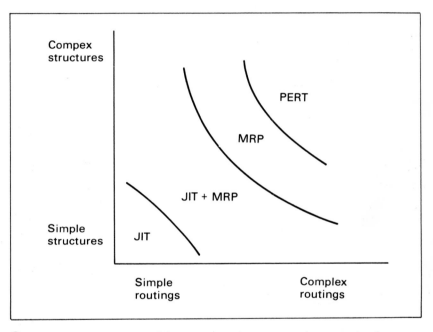

Fig. 6.6 Suitability of JIT for controlling production (Source: C.A. Voss (ed.) Just-in-Time Manufacture, p. 209, IFS Publications, Bedford, 1988)

- Reduce the amount of investment in automation required.
- Change the nature of the automation required. For example one principle of JIT is to choose many small machines rather than one large one.
- Release capital through WIP reduction to pay for some or all of the automation.
- Reduce the need for computer integration; a JIT plant is physically integrated.

What fundamental changes do we need to make, to turn our company into a JIT company?

Top management must be aware that this is not an easy road. There are many things embodied in the traditional way of manufacturing which conflict with the requirements of JIT. It is not surprising that the main resistance to JIT often comes from middle level management and technical specialists who are constrained by today's methods of management. There are four areas where a company must change, as follows.

Measures of performance

JIT demands a new look at measures of performance. Traditionally companies have tried to maximise output and machine utilisation. In a JIT environment, the short objective is to meet planned output (and not exceed it), and to use under-capacity scheduling, which may result in having planned spare capacity. In a JIT company it is important that in addition to measures of productivity and cost, management focuses on the following measures as being vital manufacturing performance measures:

- WIP level.
- Quality.
- Manufacturing lead time.
- Distance travelled.
- Space utilisation.

Using traditional measures alone will militate against successful JIT implementation. The focus has moved away from cost minimisation to waste elimination and the maximisation of value added.

Flexibility in the organisation
To make JIT work requires considerable flexibility in the organisation. This is not just at the shopfloor level but throughout line and staff functions. Companies adopting JIT must start considering how they will make their organisations more flexible from the very start.

A focus on the doer
In implementing JIT, more responsibility is pushed down the line to operators and their supervisors. They are closer to how things work and the associated problems. For example, many companies have built small self-contained cells or modules. Within these, the team members have wide-ranging responsibility for organising their own work, quality control, maintenance and repair of their own machines and movement of material to and from their cell. Tasks which have been traditionally performed by staff and/or indirect functions are now performed by the doers. Delegation from specialists (IEs, quality inspectors, etc.) should be enforced wherever possible.

Continuous improvement
The traditional focus of manufacturing management has been problem solving. Although most companies are fairly good at this, once a problem is solved they tend to leave well alone. In a JIT company, the focus changes to continuous improvement. When a problem is solved we must seek to improve still further; we are always searching for further ways to eliminate waste. JIT is a journey of continuing improvement.

These are four fundamental changes in the ways companies operate, and have been achieved not only in Japan, but by a number of UK companies. They require a major commitment by the company at all levels. Once achieved, these new ways of managing allow for new orders of magnitude of performance.

Laying the groundwork

Based on the experience of Japanese companies, JIT takes most firmly when the preparations are most thorough. Everyone in the organisation who is likely to be affected, needs to be aware of what is happening and why. Among key preparatory steps, says Professor Yamashina, are:

- There needs to be top management commitment, involvement and leadership.
- There must be the assignment of competent people and money to the project.
- There must be massive education and training to give the basic and necessary knowledge to the people concerned.
- The housekeeping must be improved to root quality consciousness in the peoples' minds.
- Statistical quality control must be implemented.
- The principle of on-the-spot investigation must be accepted and carried out by everybody in the company.

These points are all supported by the experience of companies in the West.

The necessity for *top management commitment* is expressed well by Richard Hall of Beaver Machine Tools in the UK, who describes his company's experience in these terms:

> *We learnt that JIT looks upon every section in the manufacturing environment as a supplier to the assembly shop. Management is there to help make suggestions, remove inter-departmental obstacles, push, ease, and motivate, but the foremen, supervisors, suppliers and even storemen, must feel responsible. The biggest, and most critical, step in implementing JIT is this transfer of responsibility and, with it, authority. It is sometimes equally hard for management to let it go, as it is for the intended recipient to accept it. A climate of trust, respect, credibility, and co-operation are essential.*
>
> *The climate is the responsibility of senior management and without their support JIT is impossible. It is a philosophy and an attitude of mind that must filter from the top downwards. To try and begin at the middle management level is courting disaster. JIT, like a foreign language, is hard and difficult to adjust to. Unless one is fully committed there are times when it is easier, from the short-term point of view, to ignore global issues and revert to the native tongue. If middle management are seen to be the sole advocates of JIT then the two ends can easily combine to cut them out.*

The *quality and quantity of resources* put into the project also says a great deal about the level of commitment. To change truly the way the organisation functions, the best available people need to be seconded, not simply people who happen to be available at the time.

The main costs of a properly resourced pilot are those associated with releasing and training the people who will plan and be involved in the implementation. The investment required will depend very much on the nature of the pilot. An example is a large-scale pilot at John Deere in the US involving set up reduction in a press shop. The investment was:

Die cart	$156 000
Common die plates	$183 900
Die rollers	$ 14 000
Press modifications	$ 48 000
Total	$501 900

The savings were:

Labour	$ 69 000 p.a.
Reduction of inventory	$231 840
Increased capacity	$232 000 p.a.

In practice most pilots will involve far smaller investments.

The cost of a full-scale JIT programme will depend on where the company starts from, and the size and nature of the operation etc. One example of the investment is the major investment by a Canadian car assembler. In addition to the people and training costs, the investment was:

Equipment	$1 200 000
Consulting work and engineering	$ 125 000
Equipment installation	$ 300 000
Downtime, learning curve etc.	$ 100 000
Total	$1 725 000

Education and training are the backbone of a JIT programme. They are aimed both at providing new skills – technical, problem solving, team building and so on – and at changing attitudes. In many ways, the latter is the hardest. An example of this is the pattern of support and training required for JIT in smaller companies developed by the University of Warwick.

One of the most visible aspects of Sumitomo Rubber's acquisition of Dunlop Tyre was its immediate stress on *good housekeeping*. Employees were obliged to clean up their working areas, paint the machines and walls and ensure that piles of boxes and components were no longer left to litter gangways and corridors. The raising of the working environment in this way had an immediate impact on quality of production.

Statistical quality control (or statistical process control as it is also known) is part of the basic groundwork of problem analysis and resolution. Many companies have been greatly surprised at how rapidly supervisors and operators have taken to the concept and used it as part of their normal working processes.

To get these basics underway, you will need to establish a formal project organisation, with the responsibility to plan and implement the necessary changes. A typical organisation might be:

- *Steering committee*. This is a cross-functional group of personnel who meet regularly to set objectives for and to direct and monitor the implementation programme. It includes representatives from design, purchasing, quality, manufacturing, marketing and personnel. It could well include shopfloor representation.
- *Project manager*. It is beneficial to appoint a full-time project manager to act as 'project champion' of the implementation programme. His or her duties include publicising the programme, training, facilitating meetings and 'fixing' money and resources.
- *Project team*. A common form of managing JIT implementation is to set up implementation teams. These teams may well be shopfloor based, rather than a head office firefighting team. The project manager helps to set up these teams and to establish terms of reference. Teams should be cross-functional, but related to the particular techniques being implemented. Teams should be given total backing to implement change without delay; this is the spirit of JIT.

   The teams need to be trained if they are to be effective. Methods of training commonly used include visiting successful users, using consultants for in-company courses and/or courses run by institutions.

The problem of where to start has frequently been answered by choosing a small cell or unit, and once this has been made to work, rapidly transferring the skills and experience round the organisation. This approach was used in Japan when JIT was being introduced and is being used by many firms in the West such as IBM. IBM argues that the first site should be one where success can be expected, one categorised by a stable manufacturing environment. However, this should not be seen as an ad hoc approach. The initial JIT cell should be the first stage in a long-term plan for implementation.

To build on the experience of this pilot, the company should feed the lessons learned into a few more pilots. At this stage, it should be in a position to develop a strategy for a total move into JIT.

This is a critical stage in a company's JIT strategy development. Quite often the company reaches a plateau, from which it is difficult to move on without a company-wide JIT programme. This is much more difficult to implement, because it requires the full involvement of the whole company, not just the commitment of a few enthusiastic

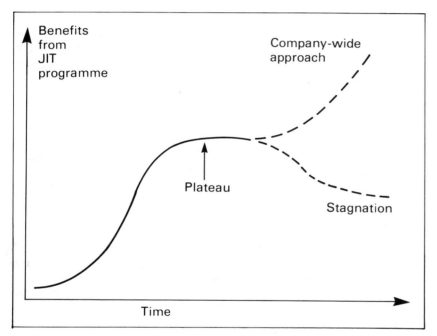

Fig. 6.7 JIT – getting beyond the
plateau

individuals. Without this two stage process of learning from the pilots, and developing a company wide approach, a JIT effort runs the risk of stagnating or even going into reverse, as illustrated in Fig. 6.7.

A good example of the JIT planning process at work is the Daventry plant of Cummins Engine, where Cummins managers and engineers formed a joint project team with consultants from PA. They were given the demanding objective of reducing floor space by 30% whilst increasing output by 70%. The planning process had to take into account four major problem areas, described by the consultants in these terms:*

Production
A high percentage of recorded lost time was spent looking for parts, transferring parts between engines, or retro-fitting parts which had not arrived on time. Labour was willing and flexible and was moved between areas to cope with the familiar end-of-month rush to complete and ship engines.

Materials management
Lead times for the high value parts were up to three times the delivery lead time demanded by the customer. In-house lead time, between receipt and delivery to point of use, was typically three weeks but could be reduced to two days by expediting.

*JIT Planning and Implementation by Keith Nimmo and Neil Reed, PA Management Consultants, London, *Just-in-Time: An Executive Briefing*, J. Mortimer (editor), IFS Publications, 1986.

Sales
Demand, in terms of volume and mix, was predictable, but forecasts were optimistic. Cummins Engine views customer satisfaction as being of the highest priority, and customers frequently took advantage of this by over-ordering, slipping orders and changing specification at the last minute.

Engineering
The variety of parts was not excessive, but to achieve customers' precise requirements the combination of these parts resulted in little commonality between engines.

To tackle these issues in a coherent manner, the project team identified four key concepts. These were, again in the consultants' own description:

- *The drive concept, which would describe how the assembly operation might be schedule to satisfy both customer and supplier delivery requirements.*
- *The build concept, which would detail the facilities, manpower, methods and organisation required.*
- *The materials concept, which would detail the in-house and external materials logistics, systems requirements, and storage media for each part.*
- *The layout concept, which would show the location of all facilities, services, access points, and storage facilities to satisfy the requirements of the above.*

All four concepts were developed simultaneously, since each was dependent upon the other three. To avoid attempts to 'optimise' one particular facet of the overall concept, continual reference to the objectives was found to be necessary. Within each, a range of options was developed, discussed, tested (often using computer modelling techniques), and rated against the objectives. Successful options could then be costed, and the risks assessed before acceptance.

These procedures threw up a number of options in terms of optimum scheduling, materials, building and facilities layout. These were all tested against the original objectives and basic criteria such as:

- *Finance*. Return on investments, capital expenditure requirement, cash flow, and so on.
- *Engineering*. High- or low-risk technology, maintenance and reliability, fitness for purpose, flexibility to accommodate new products and volumes, and so on.
- *Environment*. Acceptability to culture, corporate personnel policies, skills and manpower availability and so on.

One particularly important issue in scheduling the implementation was to achieve rapid payback, both to help finance the next stages and to give the project credibility with managers and employees. Early successes are always important in major cultural changes, to gain enthusiasm and commitment. In Cummins' case, the major activities chosen to kick off the implementation included:

- Educating, training and collaborating with employees.
- Minimising manufacturing batch sizes and developing rapid changeover techniques.
- Reducing supplier batch sizes and developing delivery frequency and reliability.
- Improving the quality of supplied parts.
- Evaluating cost on a 'wall-to-wall' rather than 'unit' basis.
- Designing new products to suit the marketplace and machining and assembly facilities.
- Introducing fail-safe quality systems.
- Reviewing organisational responsibilities.
- Reducing non-value-adding activities.

One area of groundwork all too frequently forgotten when the JIT steering committee is engineering-dominated, is customer involvement. It will normally be much easier to achieve JIT objectives if customers can be persuaded of the benefits to them – i.e. more timely deliveries, cost maintenance and so on. By sharing your JIT plans with them, you can often manage how and when they order to the extent that unnecessary fluctuations in demand become rare. When 3M's White City, Oregon, plant started to involve its customers in its JIT programme, it was able to smooth out demand to the extent that it could cut down on overtime, reduce inventory, and cope with special orders without disruption to schedules. It was also able to provide its suppliers with more accurate forecasts.

Which techniques shall we use?

A major part of the strategic and planning activity will look at the techniques to be used and the order in which they should be introduced. Successful implementation of JIT requires a number of important decisions to be made. These include what do we start with, where do we start and who should do it? There are probably more than 40 different JIT techniques and approaches. It is difficult to know where to start. It is useful to bring together the main techniques of JIT into two groups. In each group, the techniques support each other. The first group, 'JIT 1' (Fig. 6.8), is composed of the areas that are necessary for full JIT to work. They focus on four main elements of JIT that can be achieved in the short term: simplicity, flow, quality and fast set-up. Without successful application of these, further progress is difficult. In particular, quality of parts, product and process can be seen as a prerequisite for JIT. A focus of JIT 1 is the process. No

Fig. 6.8 JIT stage one

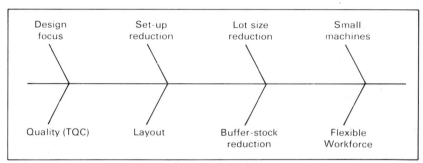

company can successfully be a JIT company without full understanding of the process in manufacturing.

Once these techniques and approaches have been implemented and assimilated, the more sophisticated and difficult-to-manage techniques of JIT can be adopted. This group, 'JIT 2', includes some of the more well-known ones such as Kanban and JIT purchasing. (The main elements of JIT 2 are shown in Fig. 6.9). Many JIT practitioners argue that JIT techniques, in particular JIT purchasing, should not be implemented until the company can handle JIT 1.

Summary of Techniques in JIT 1 (See Page 130)

- *Design/focus*. The development of focused manufacturing and design for simplicity of manufacture.
- *Total quality control*. An essential prerequisite of JIT; without high levels of quality, JIT will be difficult to implement.
- *Set-up reduction*. The reduction of set-up times so as to facilitate manufacture in small batches.
- *Layout for flow*. Changes in part layout are one of the most important and effective techniques. Changes include cellular manufacturing, U-shaped lines and moving machines together. The use of group technology can support these changes.
- *Buffer-stock reduction*. As quality improves, manufacturing flow is enhanced and batch sizes get smaller; it is then possible to reduce buffer stocks.

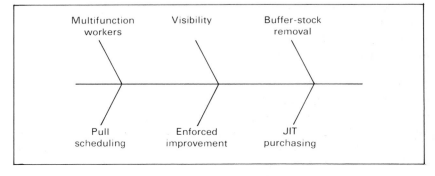

Fig. 6.9 JIT stage two

- *Small machines*. The use of multiple small machines rather than one large one can greatly facilitate flow and lead to major inventory reductions.
- *Flexible workforce*. This greatly supports a company's ability to maintain flow and low inventories when there are changes in mix and demand patterns.

Summary of Techniques of JIT 2 (See Page 139)

Having got the groundwork completed, companies can only then move on to more sophisticated JIT techniques.

- *Multifunction workforce*. Training the workforce to be able to perform a variety of skilled jobs.
- *Pull scheduling*. The use of techniques such as the Kanban system.
- *Visibility*. This involves a number of techniques all aimed at making problems visible the instant they occur, and the clear labelling of all items so that it is always clear where things are and what has to be done next.
- *Enforced improvement and buffer-stock removal*. The deliberate removal of buffers to expose problems so that they can be solved permanently.
- *JIT purchasing*. Working closely with suppliers to ensure that deliveries are of perfect quality, exact quantities and delivered in small lots when required.

Let us take these in turn.

Techniques of JIT 1

Design/focus

A key starting point in JIT is developing focus in the factory. The starting point for this is product design. The aims of design for JIT include the use of common parts where possible, developing modularity of design and designing options to fit into production flow. Toyota's guidelines for design for JIT include: 'Offer options which do not entail big changes in the heavy fabrication areas, large presses, machining and forging. These are the areas that have more difficulty in reacting to major rate or mix changes. Choice should be offered via the lighter production areas.'

To do this requires more effective communication between design and process. Designers must understand manufacturing processes and capabilities. Design teams need to be cross-functional; they must include manufacturing representation from the earliest stages. In addition, product designers may need to follow their designs through to the shopfloor. Igor Sikorski, the pioneer of aviation and helicopters once said: 'In the early days of aviation the aircraft designers were also the test pilots. This had the automatic effect of weeding out bad designers.'

Total quality management

Effective JIT requires the removal of both sources of uncertainty and variability, and of waste. Poor quality provides a major source of these. For example, poor incoming component quality forces companies both to inspect incoming parts and to hold buffer stocks to cope with the uncertainty. Both of these are wasteful. Another example is stopping the line. It can be very expensive to deal with a quality problem at that stage. The solution to the dilemma is to push quality control further back into the production cycle, and to aim for perfect quality.

In practice, implementing total quality management (TQM) is a prerequisite for effective JIT. Because the tolerance for faulty components or subassemblies is so low, quality problems *have* to be sorted out long before they reach the assembly line. TQM cannot therefore simply be applied to parts of the process; it must be functioning properly in all downstream activities. Total quality techniques should also be used in the planning and implementation for JIT itself, to minimise the disruption to production processes. 'Right first time' applies to the project management as much as to the production process itself.

This book is not intended to go into deep discussion on the merits of the various approaches to total quality management. There is no shortage of sources of advice on every aspect of quality, from design through manufacture to clerical paperwork. Some important points to make, however, are:

● Quality really *is* a top management issue. Unless top management provides a lead, it will never truly 'take'.
● Without top management support and attention, a high proportion of quality initiatives either fail or simply fade away. One of the primary reasons this happens is that initiatives are not followed through by management. Another is that the employees who suggest ideas do not get involved in progressing and implementing them. A third, and perhaps the most common reason of all, is that top management fails to *focus* innovation. By concentrating people's attention on specific issues, in a constantly evolving series of campaigns, top management can maintain the momentum of quality and process improvements over the long term.

One reason why statistical quality control (SQC) supports JIT so well is that both aim at achieving the maximum possible simplicity of product, process and operation. Anything that creates complexity – such as late deliveries, rejects or poorly functioning equipment – is a problem, which needs to be solved. By exposing and eliminating complexity, both ease the flow of production. At the same time, they reduce scrap and wasted effort.

● Quality techniques also provide the information to help suppliers improve their consistency of production. Hewlett-Packard Computer Systems Division's materials manager sees it as follows*

> You must help your supplier be successful by providing information on the product before establishing JIT. That's where SQC comes into play. We were able to provide our supplier with specific feedback on what our incoming quality inspection found compared to the quality they defined when they sent us the parts. We also collected data on the production floor and provided the supplier with this information. Without the SQC, we could only say, 'Here's the part, it's broken'. Now we can focus our efforts and the supplier's efforts to pinpoint material problems.

Set-up reduction

High set-up times result in both inflexibility and large batches, both of which are unacceptable in a JIT environment. So set-up reduction is a key JIT tool. Why does it take so long to change the settings of a machine tool? Most set-ups take far longer than necessary, because they have not been subject to a systematic analysis of what happens and what can be done to speed up the process. For an analogy, we can look to Grand Prix motor racing. If a pit-team can change four tyres in 20 seconds, why does the ordinary motorist need as many minutes to change just one tyre? The answer lies in a focused attempt to link technology, training and systems to maximum effect.

Of course, unlike the racing team manager, you would not normally wish to have a team of people standing by for most of the time, ready to rush into action for brief periods. But the same basic principle applies – a focused approach with challenging goals, where seconds count, pays off.

A practical approach to the problem will normally involve the following stages.

Analyse the causes. Many of the reasons for lengthy set-up times lie in the design of the equipment or of the product. For example, heavy parts may need to be supported while adjustments are made, or major sections may need to be dismantled. In those cases, the solutions lie mainly in redesign or in new design standards for next generation products and equipment. Much can still be achieved, however, by ingenuity – for example, could operations currently done manually be automated with a saving in time? Even with expensive, relatively modern machine tools there are likely to be additional costs of equipment to make set-ups easier.

*SQC and JIT: partnership in quality by Sarah Priestman, *Quality Progress*, May 1985. © American Society for Quality Control – reproduced by permission.

However, the mechanical problems are only part of set-up time. As Cummins Engine found when it videoed operators at work, other major time wasters are:

- The operator not knowing the job (i.e. inadequate training).
- Blunt or inappropriate tools.
- Unclear specifications.
- Lost or damaged tools and equipment.
- Awkward access to the work area (Cummins found, for example, that safety guards had been permanently welded because they rattled or had kept falling off).

The best people to identify these kinds of problems are often the operators themselves. A set-up time reduction team should therefore include operators, industrial engineers and engineering designers, who can guide each other to problems and solutions.

In Cummins' case, analysing a video of what happened during set-ups produced six basic activities:

- Clamping.
- Adjustment.
- Unclamping.
- Cleandown.
- Handling problems.
- Other.

Typical timewasters under clamping and unclamping include having too many fasteners (if it can be held accurately in place with one fastener, why use more?); inefficient methods of holding components in place (screws and bolts take excessive time to position and do up/undo); and fasteners in places that are difficult to reach (for example, out of immediate eyesight).

Adjustments give most problems when they require a first pass to check that they are correct. Not only does this waste time, but it frequently results in scrap. The ideal is not to adjust at all – to load and position in the same movement.

Cleaning time reductions involve considerations such as:

- Could we prevent the need to clean by putting in better caps or coverings?
- Could we get rid of corners and awkward shapes that require extra attention in cleaning?
- Can we clean some sections safely while the machine is in operation?

Problems need to be dealt with through further analysis to identify their root causes. Then the normal problem-solving techniques inherent in any total quality programme can be used to ensure the roots are pulled for good.

Prioritise. Which would have the greatest impact for the least outlay?

Go back to basics. If we redesigned from scratch, would we be able to take more time out at less cost? Pareto's law rapidly comes to apply in most production improvement programmes. The time to return to square one is not when Pareto begins to bite, but when the enthusiasm from the initial large gains is at its highest. At that point people will be most motivated to look creatively at the problems. The problem with going for smaller and smaller gains at greater and greater expense and effort is that people rapidly lose enthusiasm. Then the whole programme comes to a halt.

Standardise improvements. Unless the new ways of working are written down and enforced, there will be a gradual drift back towards old ways. Cummins achieve this by analysing for each set-up, which were the critical factors that made the difference. These factors were then described in detail, from how to monitor them to the specific corrective action to take for each circumstance likely to arise.

Maintenance and reliability

Whereas in a traditional manufacturing environment a breakdown can pass relatively unnoticed by the rest of the factory, within the JIT environment, a breakdown of any piece of equipment anywhere along the line can stop the entire production flow. In these circumstances, maintenance takes on a whole new role. Instead of 'fix it when it breaks', the emphasis is most heavily upon prevention. When equipment does break down, the maintenance staff must bring it back into operation in the minimum possible time.

JIT and maintenance

Among the primary implications of JIT-oriented maintenance are the following.

A change in the relationship between production and maintenance. Generally in Western companies they operate in a relationship which is at best aloof, at worst strictly adversarial. Instead, they must form a team with a common aim – maintaining production flow with the minimum of unplanned downtime. They must plan maintenance downtime together, identify and resolve recurrent breakdowns together and speak a common language to ensure that intended changes are understood by everyone concerned. Achieving this sense of teamwork is not easy. Maintenance has long been a Cinderella department, relegated to antisocial hours. The maintenance staff normally only see other staff when crisis looms. Production staff see breakdowns as maintenance's problem and, by extension, maintenance's fault. All too often, skilled work maintaining expensive and sophisticated machinery is lumped in with routine facilities maintenance. Small wonder that maintenance staff tend to be 'second-class employees'. Under JIT, however, the maintenance staff must become respected craftsmen. This requires both changes of attitude and a split between production maintenance and facilities maintenance.

Routine 'fixing' becomes the task of the operator. This inevitably requires a considerable amount of training. One of the roles of the maintenance department becomes designing and delivering the training of operators. These changes in role are major and need careful management if they are to succeed.

A change in the skill level of production maintenance staff. Even without the introduction of JIT, the traditional maintenance manager faces an increasingly difficult task in sustaining the technical competence to perform effectively in a modern manufacturing environment. Explains Colin Spratling, of management consultants, Handley-Walker:*

> *The professional role of a maintenance man in a JIT environment is that of a multi-skilled technician, merging together many traditional craft skills as well as obtaining skills in new technologies.*
>
> *Unfortunately surveys have shown that well over four out of five maintenance managers in industry, who have functional responsibility for the quality of the maintenance activity, were previously shopfloor craftsmen. Many of these maintenance managers in a medium-size organisation are poorly trained to spend very substantial amounts annually on labour and spare parts. In many organisations they are rated in the lower half of management. This degree of unpreparedness and poor skill is inappropriate to a management function whose primary role is to ensure the maximum uptime or serviceability of equipment, and whose failure to achieve this can be reflected in extensive production waste.*

In practical terms, this means that companies intending to introduce JIT must first assess the competence of their maintenance staff. In most cases, there will have to be an investment in hiring new people, probably with a significant increase in salary scale, and/or in retaining existing maintenance staff to a much higher level.

An issue which senior management will need to examine here, is whether to develop generalists, specialists, or both. To a large extent, the answer will depend upon the type of manufacture, but the trend in a large, complex production environment is increasingly towards

---

*Just-in-time and its implications for maintenance, in *JIT in Manufacturing—an Executive Briefing*, edited by J. Mortimer, IFS Publications, Bedford, 1987.

specialists who have been 'broadened out' so that they can handle other areas as required. The problem with too great an emphasis on specialisation is that the operation is overly reliant on a handful of people. At the other extreme, the 'Jack of all trades' has less and less place in an operating environment where fault finding and repairs need to be done in minutes, not hours. The two most obvious categories of specialisation are electronics and mechanical. Colin Spratling identifies the differences as follows:

Electronics. Most production equipment involves a degree of electronic control system, some of which is now very sophisticated. These systems do not lend themselves to programme of preventative maintenance but operators may be able to identify when control systems are not functioning correctly either because of specific disfunctionality, or because production features, in terms of specification, are conforming only to the outer limits of acceptance. Typically electronic faults in machinery are the most time-consuming to fix, very often because the diagnosis routine is used only infrequently by maintenance personnel. Within the JIT environment, this problem can be overcome cost-effectively by the use of spare electronic cards or spare control units, where these can be cost-justified in relation to the benefit of keeping the JIT line running.

Mechanical. Most maintenance functions are geared to maintaining the serviceability of mechanical equipment although fewer than 40% actually have a strategy for maintaining preventative maintenance policies. Preventative maintenance policies can be operated outside normal operating times. They are particularly important with mechanical equipment because in general the policies minimise the likely effects of failure and serve to report when replacement capital investments are necessary. There is a clear requirement therefore for a traditional type of planned maintenance system which focuses particularly on maintenance outside of normal JIT line running hours. The second aspect of mechanical functions is the application of condition monitoring which can very often be undertaken automatically by technical equipment. However, in a JIT environment operators are very much more closely attuned to the performance of those functions which significantly affect the running of the JIT line. Experience has shown that very often operators are the best monitors of machine operational condition.

Some Japanese companies have attempted to develop specialists who bridge the gap between these disciplines – *named, of course,* – *mechatronics.*

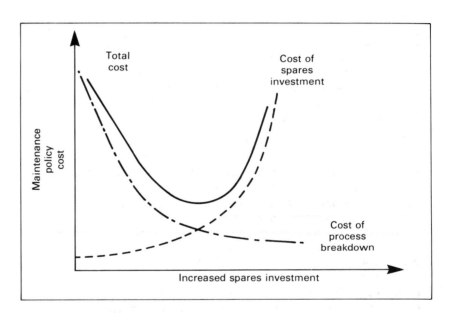

Fig. 6.10 A pragmatic approach to managing dislocation

A new attitude towards spares costs. The old story of 'for want of a nail' applies with a vengeance to the JIT environment. If non-availability of a small component can stop a machine process, it can stop the line; if it can stop the line, it can stop the factory. So spares management assumes a much more important role.

Monitoring, measuring and analysing of breakdowns provides the essential data for planned maintenace, for trouble-shooting and for spares stock levels. In many cases the latter will rise as actual and potential failures are identified and planned against. A typical cost curve for spares investment, suggests Spratling, would be similar to Fig. 6.10. The investment should, of course, be covered many times over by the reduction in costs of breakdowns, in terms of interrupted production flow.

Simulation techniques. In JIT production, simulation is used primarily to predict fluctuations in work in progress as a result of the availability and capacity of labour and plant, or vice versa. However, it also has a major role to play in maintenance planning and breakdown prevention. A simulation model can predict the impact that a breakdown in one piece of equipment will have downstream, both in terms of frequency, duration and the number of other operations affected. It then becomes possible to prioritise areas for action. In some cases, this will result in action to design the possibility of breakdown out of the system. In others, it will allow the development of viable contingency plans, and provide a valuable means of assessing the appropriate level of spares to carry. Extra training may also be needed, especially in the electronics area, to ensure that maintenance staff and operators do not replace components unnecessarily, in the hunt to identify the source of a fault.

Maintenance becomes much more involved in plant and equipment purchase, and design. It also becomes involved in design of manufacturing processes. Again, this is often a radically different role, requiring both a higher grade of skills and a new set of relationships. The new skills will include:

● Technical know-how, including the basics of equipment design.
● Advanced problem solving.
● Presentation skills – to explain to others what kinds of design changes are needed and why.

The new relationships involve building bridges not only with production management, but also with engineering and design management. This, on its own, demands a revision of the status of maintenance, because teamwork at this level depends to a large extent on each side's acceptance of the others as equals with a common goal.

The kind of changes that maintenance will seek in equipment purchase and design will reflect the need to minimise downtime. It may therefore be more acceptable to have a machine that stops several times an hour, but is restarted in seconds by the operator, than one that breaks down only once in 6 months, but takes 2 days to repair.

Layout for flow

Flow is at the centre of JIT. IBM regards it as so important that it uses the term 'continuous flow manufacturing' for its JIT effort. There are a number of steps and techniques associated with flow. The first step is the analysis of parts and their movement in order to find patterns of commonality. The first area of commonality is finding parts with similar manufacturing characteristics. A commonly used approach here is 'group technology' (GT), an analytical technique that identifies parts with similar machining characteristics. The second area of commonality is finding parts with common routings. A commonly used technique for doing this is 'product flow analysis' (PFA).

Having identified these commonalities, the next step is to look at how the factory should be laid out. GT and PFA will identify groups of parts with similar characteristics. The next step is to consider the development of small cells or modules for manufacturing or assembling these parts. By bringing together groups of parts into a cell, the distance travelled can be massively reduced and the rate of flow speeded up. Cells also provide the opportunity for developing greater flexibility amongst the workforce.

Other techniques for developing flow include the use of U-shaped lines instead of the traditional straight production line. This allows for more flexible use of the workforce. Reviewing materials handling to ensure that it supports flow is also an important tool. Finally, the simplest and often a very effective way of promoting flow is to move machines closer together. Once consecutive machines are placed beside each other flow becomes a key task, as there is no space to put any work in progress.

Small machines

In a flow manufacturing environment, using large machines in order to gain economies of scale may severely impede flow and lead to higher levels of WIP. Where the parts or assemblies from a number of different flowlines have all to be channelled through a single machine, it is worth examining the possibility of replacing the large-scale plant with a smaller machine in each flowline. The capital costs of the smaller machines may be considerably less than that of the large machine and the WIP caused by the queuing associated with it.

Techniques of JIT 2

Flexible workforce

Maintaining flow in an environment of variable mix and customer requirements requires a high level of flexibility. The prime source of flexibility in a JIT company is the workforce. Flexibility means that the workforce must be prepared to work on a wide range of jobs and be moved at short notice either on their own initiative or when required by the work schedules. For example, in a U-shaped line, the workforce must be prepared to move from one job on the line to another in order to keep the line balanced and to help out colleagues when there are problems.

Multifunction workforce

The logical step in making the workforce more flexible is to broaden people's skills. There are a number of approaches for doing this. The first is cross-training, where each member of the workforce is trained in a number of different skills. This works best if the job grading and payment systems are also reviewed. For example, in Kawasaki's US plant there are just three job grades. People are paid on the basis of the skill level that they have reached, even when the schedules require them to be working at a lower skill level. A second approach is the development of skills that are not normally associated with shopfloor workforces. For example TQM requires the workforce to conduct much of its own inspection; cellular manufacturing often delegates to the shopfloor tasks such as scheduling and maintenance, which are normally associated with management or technical functions.

Pull scheduling

Pull scheduling is often known by the Japanese description, the 'Kanban' system. Kanban is Japanese for sign, card or signal. In traditional manufacture, the trigger to manufacture is pushed down the system by means of schedules. If anything changes in the system, then pushing may lead to manufacture before a part or product is needed. In the pull system, manufacture is triggered by a signal from *down* the line. The signal can be a card (Kanban), that is returned when the previous parts have been used, an electronic signal or just an empty container. The rules are clear, nothing can be made unless there is a signal to authorise it.

Kanban is not normally the JIT technique that a company should start with, as it requires stable, repetitive demand and/or high degrees of flexibility and flow. Knowles Electronics, a small electronics manufacturer, which has successfully implemented JIT, used pull scheduling as one of the main elements of its programme. Phil Robinson, the director of manufacturing, states that using Kanban helped to eliminate paperwork, improve communication, get better control of WIP and provided a vehicle for stock reduction and quality improvement.

Visibility

This technique is often known as management by sight. Operators and managers must be able to see clearly and easily what needs to be done and what the status of production and stock should be. It involves designing systems so that problems are visible if and when they occur. One of the many detailed techniques to support this is the use of Andon boards. These coloured light displays indicate the status of each machine. When trouble occurs or before it occurs (as with condition monitoring) a red or amber light shows, summoning instant support. Another common display is a sign showing cumulative actual versus cumulative planned daily production.

Many visible systems are classified as foolproofing or 'Pokayoke' (literally translated as mistake prevention) systems. In these, the workplace is designed so that if any part of the production sequence or process is done incorrectly, it is either visible to the operator or a signal is triggered.

Management by sight also means having all instructions, schedules and other necessary documentation clearly visible to all. Kawasaki's US factory is paperless. No schedules and reports are kept on paper or on computer. Instead, they are written on boards in the factory so that everyone can see them. At the end of the month they are rubbed out. If management wants to find out what is happening in production, it must visit the shopfloor.

Buffer-stock removal and enforced improvement

Many companies carry a very high level of buffer stocks. Peter Dempsey of Rossmore Warwick identifies some of the most common causes:*

> Most companies know roughly the total value of their inventory. Few can tell you exactly where it is. The reasons include:
>
> ● Misread part numbers.
> ● Mistakes in entering numbers into a computer.
> ● Misread location numbers.
> ● Miscounted number of parts.
> ● Components 'borrowed' from stores.
> ● Suppliers delivering more or less than ordered.
> ● Genuine human error in locating components.
> ● Components in 'quarantine' or awaiting 'concessions'.
> ● Inventory control systems designed by computer-science graduates without reference to production engineers.
>
> More than once I have come across a company which has had to perform a physical stock check mid-year just to find where its inventory is. Even then one company felt pleased that the imbalance was only £0.5 million in £40 million, ignoring the fact that, typically, they found over-stocking of £11 million and understocking of £10.5 million. In other words, they did not know their actual inventory position at all.

Most companies hold buffer stocks to cover against uncertainties in quality, machine availability, schedules etc. In the implementation of JIT, a high priority is placed on removing all the uncertainties and simplifying the product and process.

However, removing these uncertainties will not in itself lead to buffer-stock reduction. This process must be managed. As quality is improved for any part or component, the buffer stocks should be progressively reduced. When quality is sufficiently high they can be eliminated altogether. The key to doing this well is to know where the uncertainties still lie and to focus on how these uncertainties can be buffered until they are eliminated.

A second approach taken in buffer-stock removal is to reduce buffer stocks progressively so as to expose forcibly problems that have been covered up over the years. This leads to enforced problem solving, as follows:

Buffer-stock removal incrementally – problems exposed – these problems are then solved permanently – further buffer stock removed – more problems are exposed – and so on.

*What goes wrong with just-in-time in the new logistics, by P.A. Dempsey, Rossmore, Warwick, UK, *Proceedings 3rd International Conference on Just-in-Time Manufacturing*, IFS Publications, Bedford, 1988.

JIT purchasing

This involves a number of important steps. These include supplier development, delivery in small quantities and at high levels of quality when required. The detailed techniques of JIT purchasing are described in more detail later in this chapter. One important consideration is that, before requesting frequent delivery from their suppliers, purchasing companies must themselves be able to practice JIT internally and in particular to be able to give stable forward schedules quickly and accurately to their suppliers.

Involving the workforce

JIT requires a commitment from every level of the organisation and companies have tried a variety of means to ensure that people do 'sign on'. Key elements of most campaigns include:

Training

Ideally, training should begin well before implementation and then be reinforced as implementation begins. It should have three elements:

● Awareness training of those in the company from top management to shopfloor.
● Training of the implementation teams and their leaders.
● Further specialist training as required by the individual projects.

The box overleaf shows some examples of course outlines for awareness training and implementation training courses developed at the University of Warwick. Additional training support can be provided by some of the many videos available.

Communications

Telling people, over and again, what a JIT programme means and why the company needs it to work, is essential to develop understanding. The most successful programmes appear to use all available media – direct discussions between senior managers and all levels down to the shopfloor operators; regular newsletters and articles in the company newspaper; videos; and external publicity (which is particularly effective in increasing people's pride in the accomplishments of their factory unit).

Once a pilot programme is up and running, it is important to broadcast its success. IBM's plant at Havant did this through a video and was gratified by the responses as JIT pilot projects started spontaneously without the need for initiation from the centre. The training sessions had provided the knowledge and had *started* to

Outline for an introductory JIT programme

9.30–11.30	JIT overview
	● Definition
	● Core JIT techniques
	● Coherent programme
11.30–12.30	Syndicate exercise: a case study
14.00–15.00	Syndicate exercise: report back and review
15.00–16.15	Implementing JIT
	● Implementing team
	● Project manager
	● Terms of reference
16.15–16.30	Seminar review and close

Outline for a JIT programe for team leaders and members

Day 1

9.00–9.30	Registration and coffee
9.30–11.00	JIT overview
	● Definition and objectives
	● Core JIT techniques
	● Implementation
11.15–12.45	Layout
14.00–15.15	Syndicate exercise: preparation
15.30–16.30	Syndicate exercise: report back and debrief
16.30–17.00	The focused factory
17.30–18.45	JIT simulation
	● Pull scheduling
	● Mixed modelling
20.00–21.30	JIT purchasing and supply
	● Preparation

Day 2

9.00–10.30	JIT purchasing and supply
	● Report back and debrief
10.45–12.00	Set-up reduction
12.00–12.30	Total quality control
14.00–14.45	JIT/MRP II
14.45–15.30	Some 'people' aspects
15.45–16.30	Course review and close

break down the attitude barriers. The pilot projects *completed* the task of changing attitudes and had produced an environment where everybody wanted, and felt able to, take part in the success that followed.

Reward systems

Two issues are of importance here. The first concerns rewards and incentives for suggestions that improve productivity or save money. The traditional suggestion scheme in Europe or the United States has not been an effective management tool – especially by comparison with Japan, where usable suggestions per employee commonly reach 20 or more each year, and frequently reach 100 or more.

The key to achieving this level of involvement in improvement is not cash incentives. The psychological rewards – recognition by managers and peers, opportunities to follow through ideas personally, and visible trophies – play a much larger role.

The second time relates to the compensation systems for routine work. Many observers, including Alan Marsden of consultants Ingersoll Engineers, point out that piecework systems are incompatible with JIT. He explains:*

> Often a company embarking upon JIT ignores the fact that they are operating a number of individual piecework systems. This directly contradicts the Just-in-Time philosophy in that it encourages the production at any cost, and ignores the requirements of quality. Piecework systems encourage high compensation for production interruptions and downtime. Although initially designed to protect earnings, they have become the means by which to achieve high earnings at the expense of production. They may have satisfied an obvious immediate need to improve productivity – but they discourage flexibility, quality and commitment and encourage time disputes, stock turns and downtime.

One of the key motivators for people to implement JIT is developing a feeling of ownership. Take, for example, Land Rover. This company did not impose JIT from the top nor did it bring in consultants from the outside. Rather, it charged individual supervisors with learning about JIT and developing and implementing plans for JIT cells in their area. This not only resulted in successful JIT implementation, but also in highly motivated teams on the shopfloor. These teams felt that they owned the JIT implementation. A similar pattern was used in the Cummins set-up reduction programme described earlier. The videotaping and the development of the improvements was done by the shopfloor team, and the video became their property. They then owned the resulting changes.

*Just-in-time – a people driven philosophy, by A.W. Marsden, Ingersoll Engineers, UK, *Proceedings 2nd International Conference on Just-in-Time Manufacturing*, IFS Publications, Bedford, 1987.

Involving the chain of supply

Contrary to popular belief, involving suppliers in the JIT process needs to come towards the end of implementation. There are several reasons for this. One is that the production system cannot properly cope with external JIT deliveries until it has set its own house in order. Another is that you may need to spend a good deal of time troubleshooting for suppliers who have difficulty meeting the JIT targets of delivery frequency, accuracy and quality. This is difficult without internal expertise.

The starting point here is an acceptance that a system of JIT supplies involves a new set of attitudes and relationships. The aim is to provide the smoothest possible interaction between your suppliers and your production flow. Indeed, the two need to become a single integrated process as far as possible. There simply is not room for the adversarial relationships that so often characterise negotiations between large companies and their suppliers. As Peter Dempsey of Rossmore Warwick expresses it: 'Most companies depend on their suppliers for 50%–70% of the value of their product. That makes your supplier the second most important person after your customer. You come third.'

In a traditional factory environment, the relationship between production and purchasing is often neutral at best. In a JIT factory, *both* have to become involved with each other and with the key suppliers. In this new relationship, the vendor company has to trust its suppliers to the extent of opening up its long-term plans, so that they can plan ahead in parallel. One benefit of this arrangement is that supplier can advise on the best use of his product; another is that the opportunities for collaborative development become greater.

According to Karl H. Hilken,* former executive director of quality assurance at Audi in West Germany, there are eight critical steps in planning and implementing a JIT supply system.

System analysis. 'Thorough examination of all documents relevant to the section of production or to the components in question, such as drawings, specifications, production requirements, testing instructions, purchasing documents etc. to check for validity and completeness and to ensure that all conditions and instructions are clearly understood by those involved. This examination also includes the implementation of the Design-FMEA and the Process-FMEA to identify potential errors and to take necessary precautions for quality assurance purposes.'

---

*JIT: building in quality assurance, by K.H. Hilken, Audi, Germany, *Logistics World*, Vol. 1, No. 3, September 1988 (IFS Publications, Bedford).

Conviction. 'All those using the JIT system internally and externally must be convinced of the system's usefulness and advantages. It must be made clear that the production and supply process must be monitored, that the material stocks in storage will be run down and that a delivery containing defective parts can bring the rest of production to a standstill.'

Selection of parts. 'Depending on the stage of manufacture or the assemblies or components in question, it must be decided which parts are suitable for the JIT system. At this point the question of process reliability must be answered. If the existing procedure is not sufficiently reliable, tried-and-tested solutions must be implemented to achieve reliability.'

Parts analysis. 'The parts and sub-assemblies chosen for the JIT system should be analysed from the point of view of errors occurring internally and externally, experience with previous suppliers, costs, transport and supply, processing and assembly. These results must be taken into account when implementing and, later, monitoring the JIT system.'

Selection of suppliers. 'A detailed examination of the suitability of potential suppliers must be carried out separately for each proposed contract. Important points for attention here are the organisational arrangements, production capacity, reliability of production, test systems, storage facilities and effectiveness of the quality assurance system. Experience from previous dealings, e.g. dependability, expertise, quality and emergency service must also be taken into consideration when selecting a supplier.'

Research by Glasgow Business School into how JIT companies select suppliers found that price was still a predominant factor in the purchasing departments' choice. However, other factors also played a strong role. Among them:

● Ability to react to changed circumstances and customer needs.
● Consistency and quality of production.
● Flexibility of delivery.

At base, JIT companies were primarily concerned to establish relationships of minimum hassle. 'Price' is no longer defined as the unit cost at the factory gate, but as 'all-in-cost' or 'cost-of-ownership' that includes any inspection, administration of returns and rejects, lost production-flow time and so on.

In return, the supplier may receive a long-term contract, which enables him to plan the long-term investments he needs to maintain and improve quality of product and reliability of delivery.

Negotiation with suppliers. As soon as a basic agreement is reached with the potential supplier, the details of the parts to be supplied and the proposed JIT system must be negotiated. All stages of introduction, organisation and safeguarding must be worked out in detail. The production process at the manufacturer's where the supplier's components will be processed must be examined in detail. The result of these negotiations should be a partnership based on mutual trust, where the supplier is involved in planning and problem solving for the goods to be supplied.

Introduction. For the JIT system to function correctly in practice from the start, any individual potential problems must be worked through with all staff and management involved, if they have not been involved at the planning stage. Introduction must start at the plant itself. The JIT system should only be extended to the external suppliers when the prerequisites have been created and the production process is 'under control'.

Monitoring. The supplier must have his production process 'under control' to the extent that only perfect components are supplied. If the production process does not guarantee this, all aspects of quality must undergo a 10% inspection and the imperfect components must be sorted out. Records must be kept to demonstrate that the process and test systems are applied correctly and are effective. 'Audits' should also be used to monitor the system. To react quickly and effectively when unanticipated problems arise, there must be good links between the supplier and the manufacturer for communicating results and any amendments to the JIT process.

Some other important points to be aware of are:

- Effective Kanban systems can minimise paperwork between vendor and supplier. The simpler the process to release components or materials from the supplier's premises and to pay for delivered goods, the easier it will be for both sides to concentrate on the really important task of ensuring smooth flow to production.
- The delivery system agreed with suppliers should insist on the minimum over-runs or under-runs. Some suppliers, such as printers, will often claim that a certain variation in run numbers is inevitable. What they mean is that they have not invested in adequate control systems. Ideally, deliveries should be packaged in exact numbers.
- The smaller the batch sizes the supplier can produce efficiently, the more likely he is to be able to deliver small quantities frequently. If he can only manage large batches, either he or you will have to hold buffer stocks – which you pay for one way or another.
- By encouraging your suppliers to insist on JIT deliveries from their

suppliers, you are helping to encourage the chain of production flow.

- For the purposes of frequent delivery, it is generally preferable to have local sourcing as far as possible (Nissan UK has gone so far as to buy extra land beside its Washington plant, where key suppliers can build custom factories to serve Nissan's assembly lines.) Nonetheless, there are other ways to achieve similar results. One method, used by some Japanese manufacturers, is to establish clusters of remote suppliers, who can share delivery facilities. In Japan, because of the very poor transport system, local really means local. However in the West, where roads are excellent, local means anywhere within 1 day's drive.

In practice, you will want to examine the options closely on the basis of:

- Will the supplier's production processes guarantee that the product is ready for despatch as soon as it is needed?
- Can the supplier guarantee delivery within an acceptable time variance?

- To make JIT supplies work, you will need to spend a considerable amount of time and effort working with suppliers, helping them upgrade their systems and procedures, and matching their production routines to yours. There simply is not the time, in most cases, to expend this effort on large numbers of suppliers. You therefore need to go through a strict qualifying exercise that focuses on:

- Identifying the range of options for selecting long-term *partners*.
- Examining their ability to come up to the level of consistency and reliability of product quality and delivery you need, i.e.:
  How willing and committed is the company to do so?
  Does it have the financial resources to make necessary investments?
  How much of your time/cost will be needed to coax it along?
- Requiring them to demonstrate performance at that level.

In effect, the qualifying process is like a series of examinations. After each successful test, the nature of the relationship between the two companies can become stronger and closer. The aim, however, is to end up with at most a handful of suppliers for each product or service that you buy in.

- Do resist the temptation to buy up specialist supplier companies in the name of vertical integration. It is unlikely to lead to improvements in production flow – quite the reverse, because the deflection of management attention and effort on both sides takes the eye off the ball.
- Do not expect suppliers to act as your warehouse. That simply transfers a problem from under your control to out of your control. The goal of JIT is to reduce inventory at all stages in the production

flow, in the supplier's production processes as well as your own. Peter Dempsey again:

> *Many suppliers from the early JIT projects thought that the major manufacturers were simply trying to shift the burden of carrying inventory cost on to their suppliers. Adopt a different attitude and you can share a common goal. Neither party need carry much inventory. Remember that the supplier too buys in 50%–70% of his product value.*

● Do not initiate competitive bidding for currently assigned components at the end of a contract period, unless you have good reason to be dissatisfied with the current supplier. The costs of bringing a new supplier up to speed are likely to be much greater than helping the current one overcome minor problems. For new components, however, it still makes sense to allow competitive bidding – too close a relationship can be as bad as being too distant.

Vital support functions – finance and management information

Traditional cost management systems do not support JIT adequately. Indeed, their focus on direct labour costs and return on investment may be counterproductive to a production system where labour costs are a relatively small part of the product cost and where multiple small machines may be more desirable than a single large one. As Keith Williams and Paul Taylor of Coopers and Lybrand explain:*

> *The primary reason why traditional cost management systems are inappropriate is that they do not recognise the changes in manufacturing focus. The JIT philosophy is built on criteria such as simplified manufacturing, product and material quality improvements, little inventory and visible control and performance indicators, whereas traditional cost management systems were designed to focus on the control of a complex manufacturing environment.*

Some of the changes in focus involved are described in Fig. 6.11. What they amount to is a reorientation from looking back at costs incurred to looking forward to how costs might be held down in the future. As Williams and Taylor explain:

> *The accountant needs to provide more support to the product and process designers in order that cost behaviour is fully understood at the design and development stage, where the most important*

---

*The impact of JIT on financial management, by K. Williams and P. Taylor, Coopers and Lybrand, UK, *Proceedings 3rd International Conference on Just-in-Time Manufacturing*, IFS Publications, Bedford, 1988.

Cost management area	Traditional	JIT
1. Control of direct production resources	Focused on the control of direct labour	Focused on all production resources, especially materials
2. Product cost build-up	Summation of numerous labour and overhead rates applied to each operation performed	Based on costing at a cell level which can be as simple as a cell throughput time multiplied by a cell rate
3. Control of production overheads	The method of allocating, apportioning and recovering overheads does not attempt to establish relationship between costs and their causes. It is an accounting exercise	Overheads are controlled at their source using such methods as the 'cost drive' approach which relates cost behaviour to causal factors identifiable in products and processes
4. Accuracy of product costs	Refined during the manufacturing process	Refined at the design stage – before the product is produced
5. Recording of scrap and rework	Complex systems are utilised to record, value and report scrap and rework	As quality improves, the need for system to report scrap and rework diminishes
6. Performance measures	Primarily based on financial variance analysis	Visibility and non-financial measures are used
7. Important performance measures	Labour efficiency, material usage, overhead recovery, cost centre control, etc.	Quality measurement, machine/cell utilisation, cell contribution/ profitability, etc.

Fig. 6.11   The changing focus of cost management systems

cost decisions are made. As product life cycles become shorter, providing support when the product enters manufacturing is normally too late to influence product costs significantly.

Because JIT forces companies to focus attention on those activities that do not add value and are therefore waste, JIT-oriented accounting processes aim to make waste apparent. (Traditional cost accounting assumes that there will be a percentage of waste and so effectively hides it from analysis.) One useful technique is to apportion overheads according to production lead time: this puts even greater pressure on production and maintenance to keep set-up and queueing times to a minimum.

A bonus of JIT-oriented accounting is that it can cut substantially the costs of management controls. Because JIT simplifies complex systems, the amount of paperwork, data gathering and calculation time can be radically reduced (see Fig. 6.12) – one large company cut its overall expenditure on management control from 4% of turnover to just 1%. The savings occur in part because so many stages of the traditional production cost control system disappear. For example, purchase requisitions, purchase orders and supplier statements become obsolete.

The same general principles apply for non-financial management

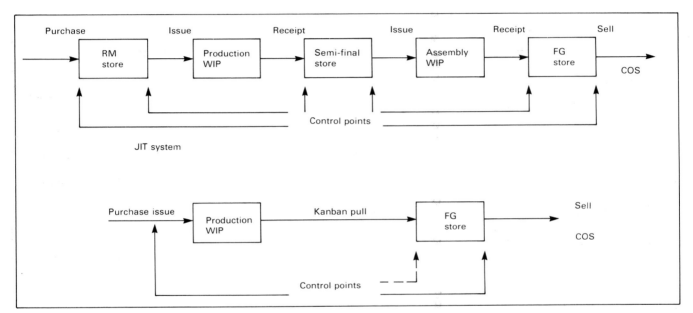

Fig. 6.12 Simplification of control
through JIT

controls. By simplifying the production process, JIT simplifies the controls, making them easier to gather and to interpret. Some of the measures will already be part of the production routine, but these will normally assume a higher priority under JIT. Among them:

● Percentage rejected production.
● Cell throughput and linearity against plan.
● Number of machine/cell breakdowns.
● Labour presence and absenteeism.
● Production cycle time.
● Cost of quality.
● WIP levels.
● Distance travelled.

Another important support area is sales and marketing. Clearly, the more accurate the forecasts of demand by the sales and marketing department, the smoother the flow of work. So it makes sense eventually to apply JIT principles to sales and marketing, too. Advice on doing this comes from Derek Slade, an associate of PE Consulting Services, who identifies five target areas for action:*

● *Operational forecasting.* Keep forecasting horizons as short as possible; take advantage of the new manufacturing lead times and production flexibility; recognise that different products have

*Asset performance – a role of JIT in sales and marketing, by D. Slade, Edward Slade Associates, in *Just-in-Time – an Executive Briefing*, edited by J. Mortimer, IFS Publications, Bedford, 1986.

different manufacturing lead times. Roll forecasts forward as frequently as practicable; do not let quarterly or yearly forecasting cycles cause shrinking horizons. Disentangle operational fore-castin-g from longer term business planning. Be sure to use relevant data for trend analysis and seek to widen the forecasting base.

● *Product availability*. Keep the product portfolio under control; make sure there is not two-thirds of the product range contributing less than 20% of revenue. Launch new products on time, and relentlessly pursue and cure the causes of lateness. Maintain a strict product withdrawal and replacement policy; do not let new products interfere with existing sales. Keep options and variants to a minimum; make them interchangeable within a product group.

● *Stocks and distribution*. Reduce the stocks in the field. Critically examine and remove unnecessary stocking points. Reduce the range of products offered ex-stock. Review central and regional stocking policies and practices. Ensure that you can provide a high level of service to your own depots and branches as well as your customers: poor central distribution services lead to excessive field stocks. Trade off transport costs with stocking costs.

● *Customer management*. Understand and influence a customer's stocking policy. Examine competitive delivery lead times and performances; find out what the customer expects. Do not provide a high service level regardless of need or cost. Segment the customer base according to factors that will influence supply policy. Co-ordinate sales activities with the stocking and distribu-tion operations. Trade off short delivery lead times with reliable delivery service.

● *Systems, procedures and practices*. Get rid of complex or fragmented systems. Reduce all computer and clerical processing times: remember information cannot be used until it is available to the next 'operation'. Relate incentive schemes and performance measures to forecast fulfilment. Measure forecasting accuracy. Eliminate informal depot management and stock control routines. Ensure that someone is reponsible for stock investment and customer service and has the authority to influence both.

Coping with setbacks

No matter how good your planning, it is rare in any change of such major proportions for managers to predict everything that could hinder progress. Part of the steering committee's role is to monitor progress, identifying practical problems before they become serious and resolving any conflicts or crises that do arise.

One of the most useful lists of common problems companies

experience in implementing JIT is provided by Peter Dempsey, as follows.*

Start-up failures
Business and strategy-related:

- Insufficient or ill-informed information on JIT.
- Lack of understanding of the business.
- Lack of strategy and direction.

Implementation-related:

- Lack of understanding of the manufacturing process.
- Lack of planning and thinking through the logistics of implementation.
- Incorrect selection of suitable product or process for initial pilot operation.
- Trying to be too ambitious in implementation (pace and scope).
- Not demonstrating success stories.

Human factors-related:

- Lack of awareness and training.
- Poor communications.
- Lack of participation and involvement of the people concerned.
- Lack of commitment from management.
- Lack of discipline.

Operating failures
- Using JIT philosophy piecemeal within existing business culture.
- Lack of understanding of the manufacturing process.
- Reducing the activity of the quality department at shopfloor level too rapidly and/or not compensating for this reduction with quality awareness training.
- Continuing the age-old tradition of treating the effect and not determining and curing the cause of the problem (how many short-term, ill-thoughtout solutions to urgent problems do you have operating months or years later?).
- Not addressing the more sensitive issues of traditional, departmental boundaries, function and remote locations.
- Not changing the management structure and areas of responsibility to meet the new demands of manufacturing.

People-related failures
- Poor flexibility, out-dated restrictive practices, and inability to cope with change.

---

*What goes wrong with just-in-time in the new logistics, by P.A. Dempsey, Rossmore, Warwick, UK, *Proceedings 3rd International Conference on Just-in-Time Manufacturing*, IFS Publications, Bedford, 1988.

- Negative attitudes, poor industrial relations, and lack of leadership.
- Inability or resistance to accepting responsibility and accountability which is pushed down to the workers.
- Lack of commitment and discipline.
- Loss of faith in management's ability to manage change perceived through:
  - Parts shortage.
  - Poor quality parts.
  - Poor quality output.
  - Irrational changes to schedules.
  - Lay-offs.
  - Breakdowns.
- Above all, people-related problems are generally attributable in the end to the failure of management to communicate, inform, and train.

Logistics failure
- Failure to operate a demand-driven materials supply system in the factory, i.e. push system not pull system.
- Starting a supplier management programme before putting your own house in order.
- Failure to ensure good communication between quality and purchasing functions and presenting a united front to suppliers.
- Allowing high levels of rework.
- Poor or non-existent engineering change procedures.
- Poorly organised stores and reducing stores activity too quickly in anticipation of 'certified' supply to the point of use.
- Scheduling large manufacturing lot sizes.
- No parts rationalisation programme.
- Attempting to have parts delivered to the point of use before the manufacturing facility, the systems, procedures and experience of the organisation can cope. Problems also arise when parts supplied are not from a 'certified' supplier. Conversely, designing a layout which cannot accept delivery to the point of use limits the potential JIT benefits of the facility.
- No supplier rationalisation programme:
  - Eliminate bad suppliers.
  - Reduce total number of suppliers.
  - Source suppliers as near to the factory as possible.
  - Eliminate suppliers who will not/cannot achieve agreed quality standards.
  - Develop 'certified' supplier base.
- Failure to have buffer and/or strategic stocks in place when developing the JIT supplier base.
- Failure to change the focus of the quality function from:

- Inspecting 'quality-in' to 'quality at source'.
- Factory-related to supplier-related activities.

The solutions to all these problems lie in:

- Properly understanding JIT.
- Proper training and organisation for implementation.
- Implementing each stage in an appropriate order, without trying to cut corners, avoid the foundations or do difficult things early.

A journey without er

The effort does not stop once you have a complete JIT implementation. Like most areas of technology, JIT is constantly evolving. JIT, with its underpinning philosophy of continual improvement, by definition can never be 'installed' as say with a machine or an MRP system. It has been described as a never-ending road.

Where does JIT go next? First, even the most advanced JIT companies in the West state that they have still much to learn and to do. A good example is IBM. As it has begun to see effective implementation of JIT, it has switched the focus of its efforts into installing JIT in its suppliers, to develop a JIT-based supply chain. Once a certain level of quality, throughput time and stock level has been achieved, it plans immediately to improve on all three.

It is interesting to return to Japan, where JIT has been established longest. In many companies there, the practices and philosophies of JIT have become so firmly embedded that the companies are no longer consciously trying to 'implement' JIT. Instead they are using these practices and philosophies as the basis of continued improvement of their manufacturing. Once JIT is embedded, the resulting production system is much more simple and stable. These conditions are ideal for automation, and many Japanese and Western companies are using JIT as a necessary precursor of automation. In the call for 'simplification, automation, integration', JIT provides the simplification upon which effective automation is built. Professor R. Jaikumar of the Harvard Business School, in an influential Harvard Business School article,* described how Japanese flexible manufacturing systems were designed more simply but worked more flexibly than their US counterparts.

There are continuing new developments in JIT. For example, electronic data interchange (EDI) is being increasingly used to support JIT purchasing; and new ways are being found of linking Western computer systems (such as MRP and OPT) to JIT. In addition, new application areas are being found for JIT and JIT approaches. For example, JIT is now being explored in process industries, and JIT approaches are being used in service departments and service industries.

The pace of development is likely to continue. JIT is clearly a 'journey without end'.

Bibliography

Books

The following books represent the best in published material on Japan, JIT and related areas.

General books on JIT

Robert Hall, *Zero Inventories*, Dow Jones Irwin, 1983.
Richard J. Schonberger, *Japanese Manufacturing Tech niques*, Free Press, New York, 1982.
Richard J. Schonberger, *World Class Manufacturing*, Free Press, New York, 1986.
C.A. Voss, *Just-in-Time Manufacture*, IFS Publications, Bedford, 1987.

Specialist books on JIT and Japan

Japanese industry and manufacturing
James Abegglen and G. Stalk, *Kaisha, the Japanese Corporation*, Basic Books, New York, 1987.
Yasuhiro Monden, *Toyota Production System*, Industrial Engineering and Productivity Press, Norcross, 1983.

Set-up reduction
Shigeo Shingo, *A Revolution in Manufacturing, the SMED System*, Productivity Press, 1985.

Quality
John Groocock, *The Chain of Quality*, Wiley, Chichester, 1986.
Donald A. Garvin, *Managing Quality*, Free Press, New York, 1988.

Foolproofing
Shigeo Shingo, *Zero Inventory Control: Source Inspection and the 'Poka-Yoke' System*, Productivity Press, 1986.

Case studies, conference proceedings

Yashiro Monden (ed.), *'Applying Just-in-Time', the American/Japanese Experience*, Industrial Engineering and Manufacturing Press, Atlanta, 1986.
Richard J. Schonberger, *World Class Manufacturing Casebook*, Free Press, New York, 1988.
C.A. Voss, *Just-in-Time Manufacturing, Proceedings of the 2nd International Conference*, IFS Publications, Bedford, 1987.

Glossary

AGV. Automatic guided vehicle; a vehicle or transporter that moves parts or products by central computer control.

Backflushing. A method of calculating stock usage that can be used in a JIT environment. Rather than count all parts issued to the shopfloor, the daily output is used to calculate what parts must have been used, these are then debited or 'backflushed' from the stock record.

Cellular manufacture. Grouping a number of machines in a cell to manufacture a set of parts with similar routing and manufacturing characteristics. Often designed in conjunction with group technology.

Family of parts sourcing. The purchasing of a family of similar parts from a single source so as to gain technical and volume benefits.

Group technology. An analytical technique, that originated in Russia, to identify groups of parts with similar machine characteristics. These groups of parts can each be manufactured using cellular manufacturing.

Heijunka. Approaches to levelled and balanced production.

Jidoka. Stopping of the production equipment, automatically or by the worker, when abnormal conditions are sensed or occur.

Just-in-time. A Western term used to describe Japanese manufacturing practices. There are two usages. A narrow view: manufacturing or purchasing parts in small numbers just in time to be used by the subsequent operation. The second usage is the broad view: a methodology which aims to improve overall productivity through the elimination of waste and which leads to improved quality. It provides for the cost-effective production and delivery of only the necessary parts, in the right quantity at the right time and place, while using the minimum of facilities, equipment, materials and human resources. It is accomplished through application of specific techniques which require total employee involvement and teamwork.

Kanban. The Japanese for sign or signal. The Kanban system is a method of using signals, usually a Kanban card, from a downstream process to trigger production of the required parts in an upstream process or supplier. This is known as pull scheduling.

MRP. Materials requirement planning: a production planning system that translates the master production schedule into a time phased statement of manufacturing and purchase requirements. It is a 'push' rather than a 'pull' system.

MRP II. Manufacturing resource planning: an extension of MRP to include planning of all manufacturing resources, not just materials.

Muda. Literally translated as waste. Anything that does not add value.

Mura. Irregular, uneven, inconsistent.

Muri. Unreasonably excess work, excessive or strained performance.

Nagara. Smoother or balanced production.

Optimised production technology. A scheduling system developed by Israeli Eli Goldrett that focuses on scheduling around bottleneck resources.

Piece part. A component part of a finished product. A unique item to be manufactured.

PERT. Programme evaluation and review technique: a network planning technique used for planning and controlling complex projects.

Point-of-use delivery. The delivery by an external or internal supplier of parts as close as possible to the assembly line so that they can be transported to the line without intermediate stockholding and with minimum movement.

Pokayoke. Foolproofing. The development of foolproof devices to prevent mistakes and defects.

Pull scheduling. The triggering of production for items through a signal from a downstream operation rather than from a production schedule prepared in advance.

Rate-based production scheduling. The scheduling of production on the basis of a fixed rate output per time period, rather than an individual order.

Seiketsa. One of the four 'S's of 'housekeeping'

Seiso. One of the four 'S' of 'housekeeping' – ensuring clarity in instructions and layout.

Seiton. One of the four 'S's of 'housekeeping' – arranging things in the best possible way.

Set-up time. The time required to set-up and to changeover production from one item to another. Defined the time from the last piece being finished to the first good piece of the next item being produced.

Single-sourcing. Purchasing an item from a single supplier only.

SQC. Statistical quality control: the use of statistical techniques to measure and control the quality of processes.

Supplier certification. A process whereby a customer certifies that a supplier has the necessary level of process quality and quality management so that incoming quality control is not necessary on its parts.

Supply chain. The chain of supply starting with the supplier and continuing through the various intermediate manufacturing and distribution stages to the ultimate customer.

Total productive maintenance. An approach to maintenance that goes beyond traditional, preventive maintenance to include involvement of the operations and broadening of the role of maintenance engineers.

U-shaped lines. Small production line laid out in a U shape so as to maximise the ability of the operation to deal with variation in mix on the line.

Under-capacity scheduling. Scheduling a plant or a line below the level of capacity of its physical equipment, so as to allow for flexible response to mix on volume changes and the solving of quality problems.

Visible production control. Making it clear to the operator through simple visible means, rather than written schedules and procedures, what work is to be done next.

WIP. Work in progress.